RICHER YOU

The One Habit That Will Create The Wealth You Desire

CHIKA NWAGWUGHIAGWU

RICHER YOU

Copyright © 2021 by **Chika Nwagwughiagwu**

Edited by **Nicole Amma Twum-Baah**

ISBN: 978-978-994-166-7

All rights reserved. No part of this publication may be reproduced, distributed, or transmitted in any form or by any means, including photocopying, recording, or other electronic or mechanical methods, without the prior written permission of the publisher.

It is expressly prohibited for groups or individuals to use any concept or methodology presented in this book in any training or unauthorized third party presentations, consultations, products or services without a license from the author. By purchasing this book, you agree to comply with these stipulations. The frameworks, other trademarks and services found herein are the intellectual property of Chika Nwagwughiagwu.

For further information or permission, address your request to: chikanwagwughiagwu@gmail.com

Design & Published By:
C&J MediaLab – 08164612943
or Email: mycandj@gmail.com

It is so exact, like a doctors' prescription. It made me realise I can still achieve all of my dreams.

Richer You, is a reflective piece with remarkable principles. I was looking forward to 'the one habit that will create the wealth you desire' as said on the cover and sincerely I was not disappointed. This book is a mind opener, especially in a country like ours where formal education is almost no longer the key to success.

It has changed my perspective in ways I never thought possible and I assure you it will change yours too. You will get to understand why you don't need to be dependent on another person's opinion of you or even seek external validation to be your best self.

Chika delivers this book in simple language with examples that everyone can relate to whether young or old, single or married, or even planning your retirement. As long as you are serious about becoming financially free, then this book is for you. I must confess, it is a must-read. I have read it twice already and I will definitely go back to it again and again.

Okwudili Nwagwughiagwu
CEO Evez Wigs & Extensions

I am amazed! , this book kept me awake all night, who knew a book on finance can be this interesting!

Richer You, talks about how you can harness your hidden talent and become financially stable. It does not only give you the tips for financial freedom but helps you reach it.

Chika believes that our habits be it good or bad plays a major role in our financial growth and wellbeing and I totally agree as I have found this out during the course of my career in the Banking sector and running my personal business. The book makes it so clear that your habits form your attitude and your attitude determines your altitude in every aspect of life.

The examples shared in the book are simple everyday situations that make it so easy to plug into our lives and situations immediately. What I love most are the tasks, where you have to write down your thoughts, your weakness and what plans you have to make them right.

The book covers a wide range of issues such as your mindset over and towards money and also how to command money to make it work for you. I must say, Richer you is not a book to read and forget in a hurry. It is a book that you will keep going back to, because every time you read it, you will find a new tip, and a new idea for financial growth is born in you.

Don't just add it to your library, get a copy for your loved ones as well.

Rachel Omonigho
Ex-Banker & CEO Rakel Collections

I am usually a critique, but I must confess that Richer You, gets 5 Stars!

You know, I stopped reading books like this because they all teach the principles of creating wealth that worked in well-developed nations while not taking into consideration the peculiarities of a country like Nigeria.

However, I must confess, Richer You is different. This book is interesting and talked about so many things I could easily relate to from my past experiences.

I totally agree with the concept of the power of habit and the theory of "Creating a money map". To be honest, I intend to create more than a single map to help me surmount possible challenges and strategize better towards achieving my goals.

This book shares so many principles that are so simple, yet have eluded so many financial experts. It is a compulsory text for couples so that they can be on the same pedestal and work as a team in building and creating wealth while inculcating financial discipline in their children. It is a game-changer for individuals and even those hustling on the street.

Chika, it will be a great disservice if this book does not get to every nook and cranny.

I will recommend it to anyone serious about creating wealth.

Nwachukwu Uwaezuoke,
Founder, Achieving Dreams Foundation

DEDICATION

I dedicate this book to my family, especially my mother, Emilia, and my sister, Evelyn.

Thank you for always supporting my crazy ideas. You are the reason I continue to soar

ACKNOWLEDGEMENTS

I want to use this opportunity to thank God for being my source of inspiration. For, giving me a message to share with the world and for trusting me to birth it despite my hesitations. Thank you for sending helpers every step of the way and making the journey easier than I imagined possible.

I also want to appreciate my parents, Chief Benjamin Nwagwughiagwu and Mrs Emilia Nwagwughiagwu for bringing me up with the right values, pushing me to be the best that I can be and always trusting me to make the best decisions. You gave me the freedom to live my dreams and to be the proud African woman I am today. I feel so fortunate to be your daughter.

To my mentors, Steve Harris, Sam Naike for pushing me from perfection paralysis to ruthless execution and for helping me overcome my mindset blocks.

To Tayo Olosunde for holding my hands as a fresh graduate and creating a platform that enabled me to discover my inner genius through - 'Mind the Gap'.

To Femi Darabidan and Peter D. Akhigbe for always showing up for me and raising the bar , your positivity and confidence has made a world of difference.

To Julius Omokhunu for encouraging me when I doubted myself and for helping me choose a compelling book title.

To Tunde Owolabi, Collins Uwaezuoke, for paying for my book even when it was still at the idea stage and pushing me every step of the way. Your friendship is a gift.

To Ugochi Ekpe, Nonye Ahaiwe, Susan Felix - friends turned sisters. Thanks for being there when I needed the extra boost.

To Nicole Amma Twum-Baah, for your remarkable professionalism and for editing my book and managing the pressure so well despite your tight schedule.

To Pastors' Poju Oyemade, M.C Enyadike, Collins Izevbihen, your teachings and words of encouragement kept ringing in my ears over the years to provide me with that father figure when I lost mine.

To Ibukun Awosika, Leke Alder, Fela Durotoye, Stephanie Obi, Temi Ajibewa, their books, and audio materials were a constant source of inspiration.

I also wish to acknowledge my connected family, My Edinburgh Business School Alumni, The Covenant Nation family, Sterling Family, MBT family, thanks for being my sounding board. I have learnt so much over the years.

REQUEST FOR TESTIMONIALS

Thank you for choosing my book, I hope you enjoyed reading it and found it insightful and valuable on your journey to financial freedom.

Your feedback is very important to me and other potential readers and I will be honoured to read your thoughts. please consider leaving a testimonial on Amazon. It will help me improve my work and help others discover the value within these pages.

To leave a testimonial, please follow these simple steps:

Go on Amazon and search for "**RICHER YOU**"

Go to the book's page, scroll down.

Click on the "**Write a customer review**" button.

Rate the book and write a brief comment about what you liked about it or how it impacted your life.

Submit your review and share it with your friends and followers.
You can also click the link below:

https://www.amazon.com/review/create-review?&asin=B08YK4VBV4

I appreciate your time and support.

Thank you for being awesome!

Chika

FREE GIFT!

**To say thank you for buying my book,
I would like to give you a free gift**

**DOWNLOAD THE FREE GUIDE
https://tinyurl.com/FREE-BUDGET-SHEET**

CONTENTS

Dedication	vii
Acknowledgements	viii
Introduction: What Are Your Habits?	xiv
How to Use This Book	xviii

PART ONE: THE BIG DEAL ABOUT HABITS

Chapter 1: Mind Over Money	23
Chapter 2: Do You Need a Makeover?	31
Chapter 3: Be Your Own Boss	37

PART TWO: MONEY MINDSET

Chapter 4: The Mind Principle	47
Chapter 5: Creating Your Money Map	59
Chapter 6: Think in Ink	73

PART THREE: MONEY DOES NOT GROW ON TREES

Chapter 7: Your Money Story	87
Chapter 8: Face Your Fears	97

PART FOUR: COMMAND YOUR MONEY

Chapter 9: Make Your Money Work for You   109

Chapter 10: Have You Hit Rock Bottom?   119

Chapter 11: The 1 Habit: Create Value   127

INTRODUCTION
WHAT ARE YOUR HABITS?

Your net worth to the world is usually determined by what remains after your bad habits are subtracted from your good ones' - Benjamin Franklin.

Many people believe they can fix all their problems if only they had more money. You probably believe so too. However, the truth is that without the right knowledge and habits, people who have money are bound to create more problems for themselves.

Habits are powerful because they shape our very existence and ultimately our future. They influence our health, wellbeing, and even our quality of life. To be frank, so many people know this, yet they have been unable to alter their bad habits because their brains have been wired, through repetition, to adopt a formula and sequence of action, making it difficult to change.

Habits control everything we do and may lead us straight to an unhappy ending if we do not act with tact and intelligence. Have you wondered why there are so many things we do without thinking about it? This is because we have carried out such actions repeatedly over such a long period that these actions have become second nature to us. Some habits started from childhood, others in our adult years. These habits have become so common and well known that many of us have become branded by them. Some people have even mistaken them for talents because we have refused to outgrow or change the way we see and do things. One of such habits passed on from childhood into adulthood is our relationship with money.

Very few people have spent time trying to understand their relationship with money. They get confused mid-month when they look at their bank accounts and ask themselves where all their money went, sometimes they go on to imagine there is a black hole sucking up the money in their pockets, causing everything to vanish into thin air.

Well, I would love to agree with you, but self-denial will never make all our troubles go away. Everybody thinks about making money, but nobody stops to think about what happens after we get this money and how to manage it so that we can leave a legacy for ourselves and our unborn generations.

History is rife with great men, many of whom because of their poor relationship with money and habits, went from grace to grass or, worse, had their children squander all they had amassed and wiped their footprints from the sands of time. We must remember that true wealth is not in the pounds and dollars, but in how we multiply wealth to make our lives happier and make the world a better place.

Everybody dreams about being wealthy, but very few people teach about wealth, not even our parents. The times are changing so fast that the ideas that seemed like a goldmine a decade ago, can hardly earn you a decent three-square meal today. It is no wonder that many, including parents, are at a loss when it comes to which values to pass down concerning money.

The world economy is controlled by the circular flow of money, yet our formal educational system lacks a fully integrated and established curriculum on personal finance mastery or financial literacy to guide the growing population of youths and teenagers. A curriculum that includes lessons on savings, budgeting, investing, compound interest, debt management, opportunity cost, risks, and rewards, are all necessary to prepare the coming generation and prevent them from making the same mistakes we are making today.

If we take a journey down memory lane, we will discover that we have been taught to classify learning in the form of the arts and science, except that wealth-building defies the arts or sciences. It is formed at the core of humanity through our habits and that is what this book will reveal to you.

This book will explain why even celebrated geniuses have failed to succeed at wealth creation while those labelled as misfits, psychologically impaired, dullards, dropouts relegated to the bottom of the class barrel have continued to amass wealth as footballers, baseball players, software engineers, IT gurus instead of lawyers, accountants, bankers, doctors, and economic analysts.

'Richer You' will walk you through the mental adjustments necessary to unlocking your wealth potential and dealing with your money blocks while helping you face your fears. It will help you understand and repair your relationship with money, and I will virtually hold your hand while you rewrite your money scripts and introduce you to the one habit that can change everything.

HOW TO USE THIS BOOK

To get the best use from this book, I will advise that you read each line and internalise it as if it were written for you and only you.

Read it, meditate on it, and answer the questions as honestly as possible and see how it applies to your current situation. Have your pen and paper beside you and take all the exercises with an open mind. Go over your answers again and itemize the things you need to change immediately. Execution is key to every transformational process.

Finally, write down your experience on your journey to self-discovery and unlocking the secrets to true wealth.

"It doesn't matter what your background is or where you come from, if you have dreams and goals, then it is your responsibility to make it happen"

Chika Nwagwughiagwu

PART ONE
THE BIG DEAL ABOUT HABITS

CHAPTER 1
MIND OVER MONEY

Creating wealth is a process that requires the overall wellness of your mind and body. At the top of the dimensions of financial wellness are your habits. Your habits are influenced by your beliefs, your beliefs control your mindset, and your mindset controls your ability to create wealth.

We all love to make more money, and you know what some extra cash will do for you, but I am not certain that you have considered how your emotions and thoughts can be sabotaging your desires. You can decide to read many more books on personal finance, get a mentor in stock trading, enrol in a real estate course, or even hit the jackpot right now, but if you do not believe you will ever be rich, it may never happen for you. This is simply because you will find yourself doubting, second-guessing, and passing over good opportunities to attain the life of your dreams. That is the power of the mind. For some, their relationship with money does not come from a lack of knowledge or willpower. On the contrary, most of it comes from subconscious beliefs and patterns that can be traced back to early childhood, which has given you a false lens from which you see life. It has made you believe the worst of yourself.

To put it kindly, a famous quote from Henry Ford says, "whether you think you can or you think you can't – you are right". So you are not powerless, all you need is to identify those negative patterns that are holding you back and start by correcting them using positive affirmations, then work your way up from there.

RIGHT BELIEF + RIGHT HABITS
=
FINANCIAL WELLNESS

Financial wellness is not a function of education because if that were so, then accountants, bankers, professors, and economists would be the wealthiest people we know. However, you and I are aware that this is not the reality today. What we know for sure is that the things we believe will determine what we do, and our actions will ultimately lead us to either success or failure.

Positive money habits make us feel financially well in about the same way that exercising and eating healthy makes us feel good. People only think of wellness in terms of physical, emotional, occupational, social, and environmental health. This is all good but, take for instance, a situation where you are physically unwell (sick) and, because you neglected your financial wellness, you cannot afford to see a doctor and do not have enough money to pay for your medical bills. We all know the consequences of that. This is the same for every other segment or dimension of wellness.

Financial wellness refers to your overall financial health as an individual and it entails having control of your money as it affects your day-to-day life. It means creating a soft landing for yourself by saving up some money as an emergency fund, staying low on debt, and managing your expenses to ensure that debt is only used to finance assets that can cover the cost of the loan plus interests and fees, and not to fund your lifestyle. Debt is good if it is used to create more money and income yielding assets for you.

The absence of financial wellness is the number one source of personal stress and anxiety and it has far-reaching consequences in our relationships and homes. The side effects of poor financial health include internal conflicts in the family, depression, stress-related illnesses, a decrease in creativity and productivity, and, if not effectively managed, may even lead to a display of some criminal tendencies in order to get temporary relief from a predicament that can only be cured by the right information and habits.

Financial wellness is more than a feel-good buzzword targeted towards retirement, credit score, and debt repayment. It aims at a more wholesome and encompassing experience. Authentic financial wellness is focused on mind reformation, habit evaluation, and setting a strong financial foundation, such that the individual is self-aware. As a result, he attains overall satisfaction with his current financial status because there is good reason to hope and strive for better. He has the keys to change his actual financial outcomes through the application of the right knowledge and behaviours; of which we cannot takeaway budgeting, saving, debt reduction, and an ongoing plan to reach future financial goals.

DIMENSIONS OF FINANCIAL WELLNESS

Financial wellness talks about our relationship with money and the way we interact with it in our everyday lives. It also talks about how we can deploy our financial knowledge to make informed decisions and investments and set realistic goals for ourselves and our families. Besides, it deals with what our financial values are, and our emotional awareness of how money is linked to living a purposeful and healthy life.

Overall, financial and intellectual wellness is a function of the information at our disposal and the quality of the decisions we make. They are also largely dependent on the kind of mentors we have, the books we read, the videos we watch, and our ability to analyse situations, learn from mistakes, and act on ideas at the speed of light.

It is clear by now that financial wellness cuts across our emotional, social, physical, and intellectual wellbeing, all of which can be boosted or destroyed by our habits.

For example, whether it is maintaining a sound mind, positive self-esteem, empathy, and self-care, your habits contribute heavily to your emotional and mental health. What you believe about money can either attract money to you or push it further away from you, just as much as whom you associate with determines your level of motivation.

As the famous saying goes, *"show me your friend and I'll show you your character,"*

I say, show me a man with four friends who have poor mentalities, and I can assure you that he is the fifth because I am yet to see a man rise above his closest associations or cliques.

Your physical wellbeing is equally important because no matter the amount of wealth you create, it can only be enjoyed if you have sound physical health. You may be able to afford the best medical care, but no one enjoys wealth on a sickbed, even if it is framed in gold. So, little habits like exercising and eating right is a no-brainer and if you look closely you will see that this is a universal language spoken by the rich no matter their race or the continent on which they may be found. If you can successfully change your habits, you can change your life.

NOTES

REFLECTION

DATE: | **TIME:**

WRITE DOWN YOUR THOUGHTS

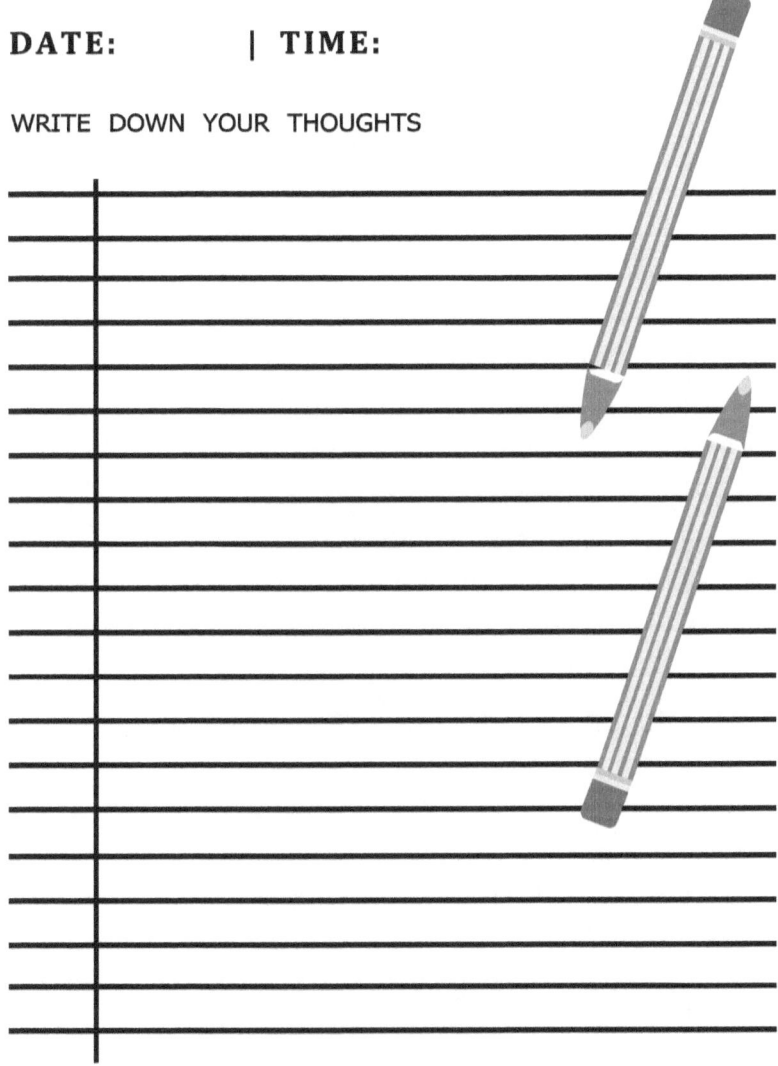

RICHER YOU

CHAPTER 2
DO YOU NEED A MAKEOVER?

I had a unique habit growing up, I loved to argue. I argued for fun, I argued to spite people, and for some, it was just to get on their nerves. I would argue when I was bored or when I simply wanted to be a little devil. It was so much fun for me; that heady feeling of going zig when others were going zag. I could go on for hours throwing facts and half-truths twisted almost cruelly, just to prove my point. Little did I know how much I had altered my personality through this habit of arguing for arguing's sake.

The thing about this habit of mine, however, was that I was so good at proving my point, it soon became my brand and almost stole my identity.

As I grew up, everyone believed I had what it took to be a lawyer, and many tried hard to sell me on the idea. They had a lot of evidence to back up their claims and I almost bought into this without asking what I wanted for my future. The only person to stop me, thankfully, before I made the mistake of choosing to study law, was my mother. She was the only one who understood me and was able to see beyond my youthful exuberance and mischief. I am eternally grateful to have such a strong support system.

You may be wondering, what is wrong with being a lawyer? Well, nothing, except the fact that at my very core, I had no interest in studying law or pursuing it as a lifelong career. Once I realized this, I had to consciously start doing things differently, and there was a myriad of things I had to stop doing almost immediately, to ensure that people perceived me in a different light.

Most importantly, I chose not to live my life based on public opinion, that singular decision changed the course of my life and today you can do the same. So many people have consistently displayed patterns and accepted labels they are not comfortable with and have easily settled for less. They assume that since everybody agrees on it, it must be the right reflection of who they are.

You may have displayed these traits out of ignorance, but you do not need to allow them to define the rest of your life. Mistakes are the building blocks of life, pick yourself up and move on.

Have you been described as a dullard at school, labelled stupid at home, bullied at work, or jeered by those you called your friends, so much that you have come to believe that you will never amount to anything better? Then allow me to hold your hands and make you understand that nobody has the right to define you. If you can allow yourself to dream one more time, you can be whatever you put your mind to. You just must believe and harness the power of the mind.

WHO ARE YOUR CHEERLEADERS?

Too many people have bad habits that they have nurtured all their lives and have never thought of a reason to change, not even for a day. These individuals have people cheering them on, and as a result, they do not see the need to retrace their steps and find out who they truly are or why they do the things that they do.

Yes, it might surprise you, but good or bad, you will always have people in your boat encouraging you as friends, well-wishers, nosy neighbours, or even as fans. The smiles on their faces and unsolicited comments from their lips give you the energy to keep moving, but unfortunately, towards the wrong direction until you get to the deep end and find out you were all by yourself the whole time.

These praise singers may have simply turned a blind eye to your faults because they do not know any better or because of the personal benefits they stand to gain. Either way, nobody can understand your goals and layout the plans for your life the way only you can.

Some are lucky to pinpoint their bad habits early but lack the willpower to correct them. So many, want to have different results but because of their habits, they find themselves on autopilot doing the same things over and over. I am quite astonished at their surprise when they get the same results. They see themselves stuck in the mud, weighed down, confused, and can see the trail of the mess they leave wherever they go, yet they make themselves more comfortable in this state rather than find a way out.

The power of habits is often overlooked but I assure you that most of our problems or successes can be traced to this simple word. If you desire a different result but you find yourself defaulting to your comfort zone, then you ought to know that something must change.

NOTES

REFLECTION

DATE: | **TIME:**

WRITE DOWN YOUR THOUGHTS

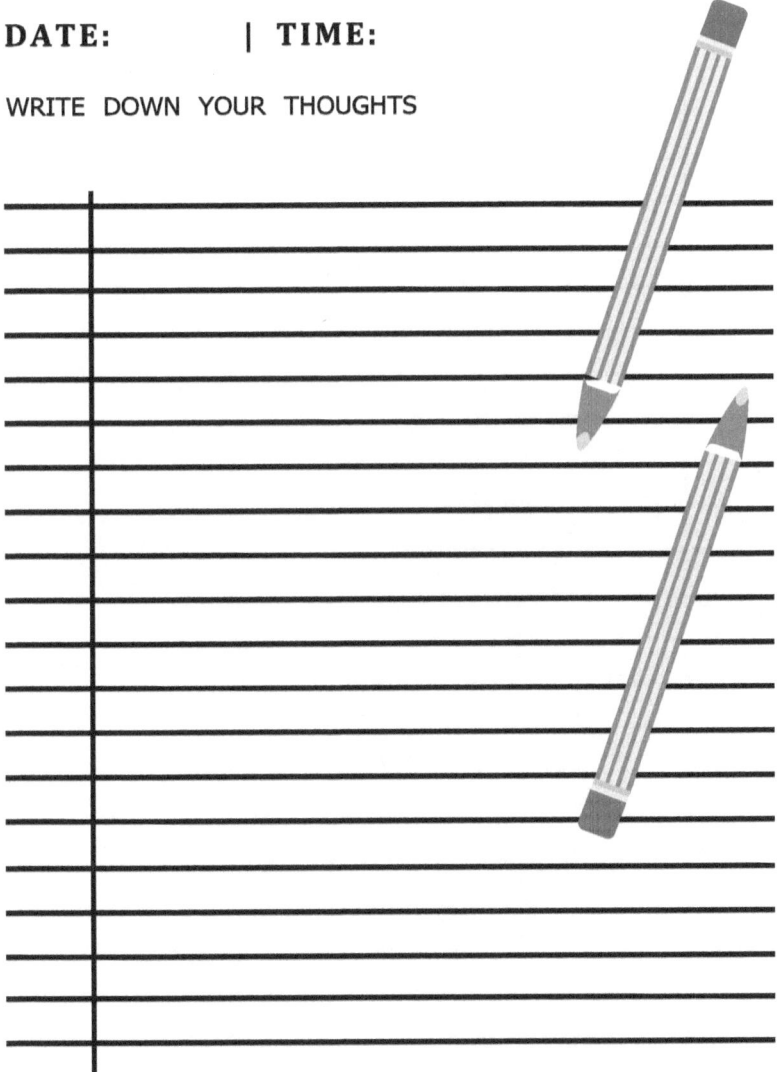

RICHER YOU

CHAPTER 3
BE YOUR OWN BOSS

To experience new results, truth be told, you must wake up each morning with a new attitude and an open mind, and with a conscious effort to embrace change. There are certain choices you must make that no one can make for you.

Most times, your mind wants something different, but because your body has been automated over some time, the reverse happens. It happens to the best of us. It is like you do not own yourself. You want better, you know better, you want the best for yourself, for your family, and your loved ones but you cannot seem to take the right steps to achieve your desires.

You long for a new experience but want to hold on to your old self. How does that even work?

"How can I stop myself from sabotaging my long-held dreams and desires," you may ask?

By being your own boss and owning your outcomes. Take responsibility! If you do not like it, change it, and act fast.

You may have tried so hard and realized that having the right desires, reading the best books, having the best mentors, or attending the best schools is not enough. Well, the only thing potent enough to compel the change that you seek is dogged determination and the power of execution.

Enough of the Aha! moments, it is time to roll up your sleeves and get to work.

Do it now, do it afraid, do it scared, but just do it!

If you are reading this book and decide not to act, you are just perhaps 1% better than the person you were before you had the chance to get this book. Act now!

YOU ARE THE SUM OF YOUR HABITS

You are where you are today not because of the economy of your country - things can only get better or worse so why focus on what is beyond your control?

Your station in life is not because of your educational background, after all, there are millions of frustrated, educated people all over the world.

You are not restricted because of the industry in which you find yourself. So many people show up every day and put in the work because of their responsibilities to their families and loved ones.

Your background is not the reason for your limitations. You can always set your own record and run at your own pace, on your own terms.

It is safe to presume that you know a few people who are labelled as 'never-do-wells,' dropouts, and misfits, and have still encountered fifty times more success through sheer determination and force of will.

Just like anyone else, your success is determined by your ability to overcome your limiting beliefs; you just have to go out of your way to be the success you want to see. Your limitations are only in your head. None of them is real until you experience them for yourself.

And even when you do, you must re-evaluate your situation and try again because you would have been given the gift of hindsight and discovered one more route to lead you to your preferred outcome. You will find that once you maintain a positive mindset, you can overcome obstacles as they show up. And even when there is no obvious, well-trodden path, you will beat down the path to your destination.

Overcome your constraints and always remember that you are good enough, smart enough, and strong enough and that these restrictions are purely in your mind. All you need is the relevant information to get you moving speedily in the right direction. This is what this book will help you to achieve.

Like so many people I know, when you hear the word habit, you will likely say or think things like 'this is who I am', 'I cannot change', 'this is the way I have always been', and 'everyone loves me this way'. Do they? But let's say, "everyone" does love you the way you are. Does that help you get from one point to a place of total fulfilment?

You need to increase your capacity in terms of knowledge, association, habits, and attitude if you are to make any real progress in your endeavours.

Let us look at the simple analogy of a smartphone. Have you ever picked up your phone and noticed a prompt asking you to do a 'software upgrade'? This tells you that to remain smart, and relevant in the future, you must consistently adapt and improve on your ability to handle challenges if you want to remain relevant. And just like the smartphone in your hand, you need to constantly upgrade yourself to reach your full potential. You need to evaluate yourself constantly and, if you check your core and realise that you are not at your best, it is time for an update.

Your actions or inactions are the reason why you have come this far. Whether you have made progress or failed, it all boils down to those little, seemingly insignificant, involuntary decisions you make without thinking about them. If you want a different result, you must change your dominant habits.

Habits like procrastination, impulsive spending, and shopping, not sticking to a budget, not having an emergency fund, falling for discount purchase temptations, trying to impress others, failing to set up money plans, spending more than you earn and fad chasing, are at the top of this list.

On the other hand, taking a firm decision to change some lifelong patterns will require a lot more than wishful thinking. It entails determination, discipline, and the ability to say no to yourself even when you crave it the most.

The trick is to imagine you are on a diet. and with every diet plan, if correctly done, the benefits will far outweigh the momentary discomfort. If you understand the fact that your perception becomes your reality, then you will paint a better picture of yourself and undergo that transformation to unlock your full potential and build habits that will automatically lead you to success!

EXERCISE

UNLEARN
OLD HABITS

DATE: | **TIME:**

WRITE DOWN YOUR THOUGHTS

EXERCISE: UNLEARN OLD HABITS

What are some habits everyone complains about but over-looks because you are charming, smart, or even beautiful?

_____
_____
_____
_____
_____
_____
_____

List those negative behaviours you think will never change.

_____
_____
_____
_____
_____
_____
_____

Are you ready to go through the transformation process?

_____
_____
_____

Take a deep breath and list all the old money habits that you would like to correct.

_____
_____
_____
_____
_____
_____
_____

Make a note of why you want to change them.

_____
_____
_____
_____
_____
_____
_____

Match a bad habit against a good habit you would like to replace it with.

_____
_____
_____
_____
_____
_____
_____

CHAPTER 4
THE MIND PRINCIPLE

It is said that the mind is filled with boundless power, compassion, creativity, and resilience. It is the tower of universal energy and intelligence of all life, even a vast reservoir of untapped wisdom if you ask me. It is the seat of success and failure. In other words, you must have first failed in your mind to fail. If you can transform your thinking, you can positively influence your outcomes.

I wish I could explain this better but let me share a brief scene with you. Have you ever sat for an examination thinking you are going to fail because you did not have time to prepare adequately, you enter the hall with so much fear that you can almost hear your heart pounding loudly?

To make matters worse, you cannot even recognise the questions because they were set from the course outline of two semesters ago. Suddenly, you have this cold feeling of despair because nothing could have prepared you for this. Unfortunately, you take the test and FAIL?

Take, for instance, another student going in to take this same test. He does not know any better than you do, but he goes in to take the test with the confidence that he will not fail. This person receives his test papers and his mind immediately gets to work and starts to make connections. He keeps telling himself, 'I cannot fail, I cannot submit this sheet blank,' and VOILA! he passes the test and cannot even understand how he did it.

One thing is certain, his success started before the test. He followed the mind principle and said to himself, as we say in Nigeria, 'I cannot carry last.' This short but simple affirmation triggers neurons in the brain cells that seek a positive outcome no matter the situation.

Wealth creation is not a function of hard work, if it were, bricklayers or masons would be among the wealthiest.

So many people have the drive and desire to make money but lack the right mindset. With such people, even if you were to drop the money into their laps on a golden platter, because of their mindset, they would self-sabotage and would not know what to do to multiply the money until they have squandered it all. Some lottery winners and those who have been gifted an inheritance are just a few examples that come to mind.

PART TWO
MONEY MINDSET

To others, money is the key to a happy and content life and a means to secure the future. The simple thought of money brings a warm feeling to their hearts and a smile to their lips.

It could also mean respect from their spouse, their kids, and extended family. It might just be the difference that makes their wife look at them with love in her eyes or disappointment in her heart.

To others, money is security. Most times, you go through your day full of worry when you remember all the bills you must pay and the fact that you do not have enough in your bank account makes you depressed. At times you ponder on all the things you could do if you had all the money in the world and how your life will be different. This feeling would probably go away if you had savings in the bank, right? This is why money means security to a lot of people as well.

For those who can meet the basic needs of food, warmth, clothing, shelter, education, and a thriving relationship, money may mean different things to them. Money could be:

- An opportunity to save a life, fulfil a purpose and add value to humanity.

- A tool to give hope and help the less advantaged fuel and fulfil their dreams.

- Passport to gain respect from friends, their communities and to be celebrated in the eyes of the world.

In my hometown, we have numerous titles to honour people in the latter category to make them happy to spend that money with reckless abandon. We call them praise-names such as okosisi 1 (The great one), osi na nwata buru oghananya (the one that became wealthy from childhood), onwa na e ti ri ora (Man of the people/ Philanthropist/ Moon that shines on everyone), akpu n wa (Strong man/ dependable), and the list goes on.

In Igbo cultural context, praise-naming is a positive reinforcement often harnessed to make people more committed to working for the public good and demonstrate personal excellence to others.

Whatever your reason for having money is, it is your sole responsibility to find it, acknowledge it, and let it push you to live the kind of life you will be happy to pass on to your kids, loved ones, and generations after.

Money is not static, it flows to those who know how to spend it, circulate it and expand it. A good example is Amazon CEO, Jeff Bezos. He is causing money to expand and circulate so fast that money, just like a current, keeps flowing back to him, making him the richest man in the world as of the year 2020. Mind you, this was still the case even when the entire world was struggling with the coronavirus pandemic. Wealthy people create jobs, empower people, build factories, give to charity, and so on because they have mastered the art of keeping money flowing to them.

Keep in mind, however, that the currency of the future is not just fiscal money but creative energy too. Creative energy is the ability to direct what you have on the inside through the right channels to create the abundance that you honestly deserve.

DO YOU NEED EXTRA CASH?

Let's complete a quick exercise by answering these questions and writing down your answers on a piece of paper or digital notepad.

Why do you need to make more money?

_____
_____
_____
_____

RICHER YOU

What will that extra dollar or Naira in your account do for you right now?

Which pressing needs do you sincerely wish will be taken care of or sorted out for good?

Do you want a vacation, a new course, or even better schools for your children?

What did you discover? Hopefully, you discovered what you genuinely want for yourself. I also hope that you feel deserving of the things you wrote down. If you do, congratulations; you do! So, by all means, go for it!

When you understand the type of life you want and the kind of person you want to be, all there is left to do is work on the habits that will cultivate you into that person.

The key takeaway is to discover what money means to you and to develop a personal relationship with it. Recently, I sent out a survey and received over a hundred responses. In those responses, no two individuals had the same purpose for money or understanding of money. Money means different things to different people, so do not always assume that everyone has the same basic needs.

WHAT DOES MONEY MEAN TO YOU?

Money means different things to different people. Until you define what money means to you, you will never push yourself to be more, to do more, to accomplish more, and to live the kind of life you truly deserve. To accomplish finding your 'why,' you must be willing to stop living according to the dictates of other people.

To some, money makes the world go round.

Money is value and a measure of wealth and standards, a boost to people's self-esteem and egos.

Money is also a medium of exchange for all the beautiful things people want to acquire; a new house, a new car, a vacation to the Bahamas, the latest iPhone, new shoes, and beautiful clothes, the list is endless.

For employees, money is a reward for a job well done as well as payment for using time and energy to accomplish a task for their organisation. The idea of a great place to work is often a fat cheque at the end of the month.

Money can also mean financial independence and the ability to meet all your expenses without being dependent on anyone for the rest of your life or taking orders from anyone.

EXERCISE

LETTER TO
MY FUTURE SELF

DATE: | **TIME:**

WRITE DOWN YOUR THOUGHTS

EXERCISE: LETTER TO MY FUTURE SELF

I have just one activity for you here. I want you to write a letter to yourself.

Tell your future self how your life would be different if you had all the money in the world. List the honest steps you would take to achieve this life. Then read it out loud and repeat it to yourself until you can visualise it and it all starts to make sense to you.

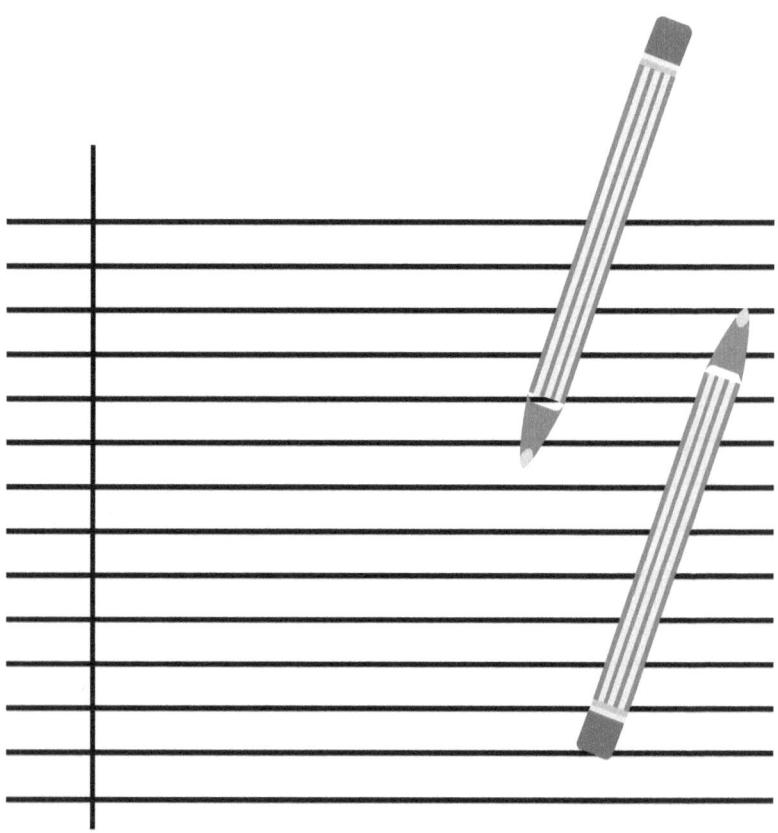

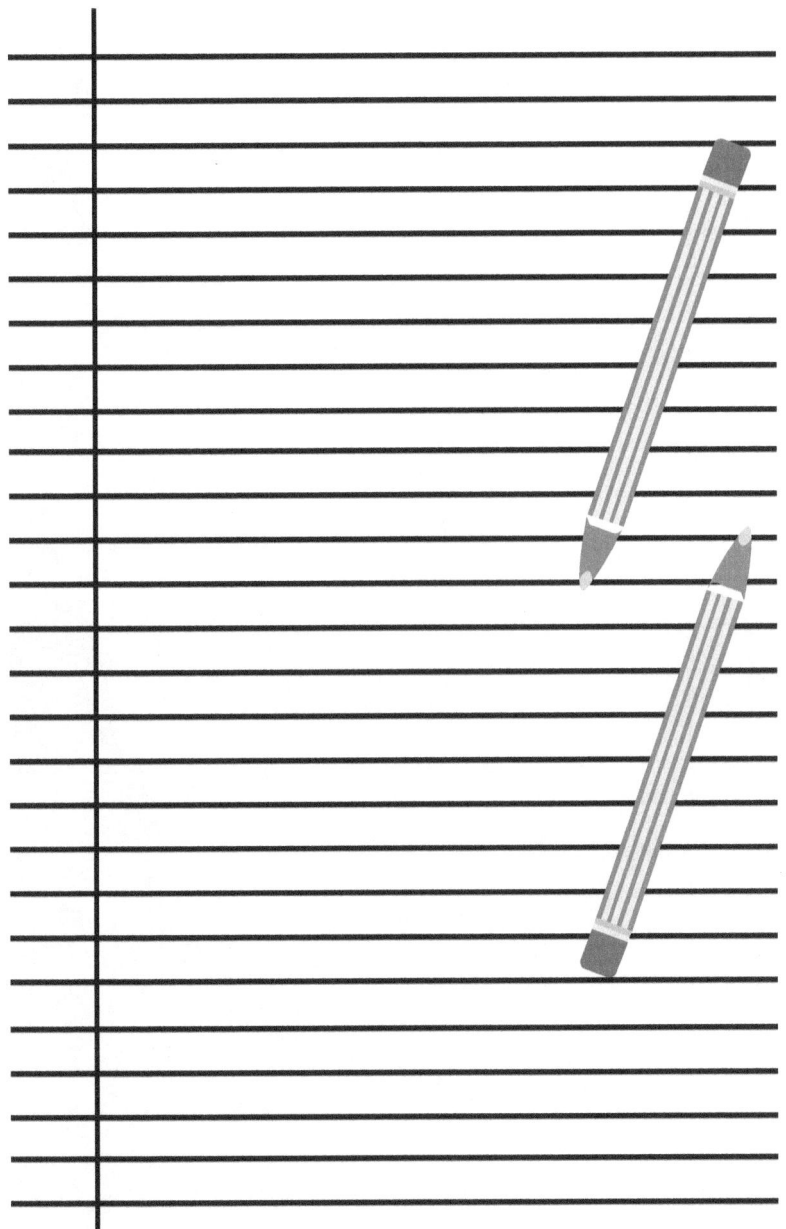

RICHER YOU

CHAPTER 5
CREATE YOUR MONEY MAP

"On your Marks, Set ... Go!"

Imagine you are on a trip to a destination you have never been before, and you do not have a guide, a map, or compass to lead you there. How will you feel? Lost, confused, afraid of missing your way? At what point will you realise that you are totally off course, and what steps will you take to get right back on track?

To get to your destination, you must make a clear decision on:

- where you want to go.

- how long it will take you to get there.

- the resources that will sustain you while you are at it.

- roadmaps, and a landmark so you can identify it once you get there.

Ultimately, you must paint a clear picture of what your destination will look like. Next on your list should be to move your plans from a mind map to a vision map to gain better clarity of your destination.

WHY VISION MAP?

You may have heard of vision boards in the past, or it might be a new term to you. Either way, vision maps, or boards, as they are more popularly known, involve putting together a collage of images and words to represent a person's wishes and goals and arranging them on a board to serve as a reminder of where they are heading. These pictures often serve as a source of inspiration or motivation, but vision boarding is never enough.

A vision map does not only represent your goals and aspirations; because wishing for something is never enough to make it happen. It goes further to analyse the pathways, skills, energy, and resources that you will need to get there. It tells a story of the step-by-step journey you will need to take to achieve your goals. It helps you envision the entire process and once you can visualize it clearly, then you will never miss it and that clarity will help you pick up on speed such that you will fly high like a shooting star.

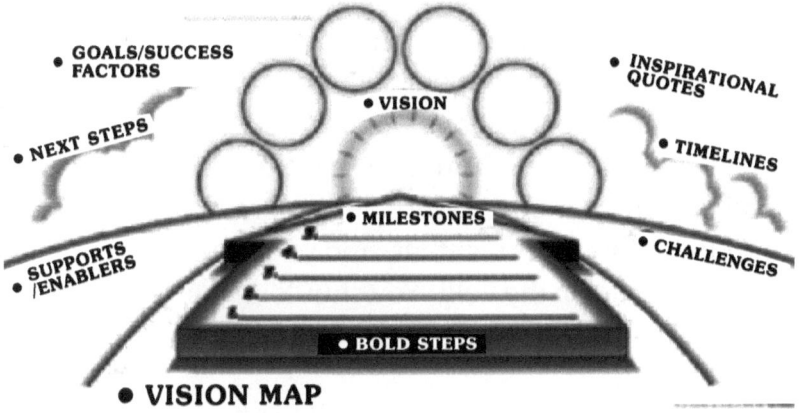

Copied 2017 Lizard Brain Solutions

On your road to uncover true wealth, there are also important questions to ask yourself, important decisions to make, and a clear picture of what a 'richer' you will look like so that you will recognise it when you become it. This process is important and the closer you get to your goals, the clearer the picture will be in your mind's eye. So, it is okay if you cannot answer all the questions from the starting point. Your vision map is a working document and can be updated and reviewed to align with certain realities as you go.

If you do not have a goal, you will never know when you have reached the finish line. There must be the desired result you want to reach or attain. This will serve as your guide to know when you reach your desired destination. Get a clear direction of where you are going and steps on how to get there, the strategy or tactics to get you there, and keep your eyes on the price. Close your eyes for a moment and imagine a game of soccer. You are at the stadium and you have bought a ticket to watch your favourite team play. You have a front-row seat, a drink and popcorn in your hands, your family at your side, you love the sunny weather, and you have a clear view of the players on the field. You should agree with me that nothing can go wrong on such a beautiful day as this.

You watch the players as they file out of the dressing room, the best of the 11 players featured in each team all energised to kickstart the tournament, and you are already cheering for your team and calling them by their nicknames as if you have known them all your life.

Then, just as the teams have gathered on the field, you realize that there is no goal post.

So, you have the best of the best, smart, athletic, energetic, skilled players chasing a ball endlessly for 90-minutes with no clear purpose in mind because without a goal post, there is no place to shoot the ball into!

Frustrating, right? Wasted time, effort, skills, and maybe even some injuries picked up along the way but no goals to aim for.

That is what it looks like when you are trying to manage your finances without setting clear and simple goals or paying attention to your money.

You wake up each day, rush off to work, queue up in traffic, get home drained and stressed out and after all this effort you live paycheck to paycheck cursing and blaming everyone but yourself. You hold on to wishful thinking, praying that it will all work out in the end.

After you design your vision map correctly, you will see that you can almost reach out and touch your goals because you know the next steps and can see your plan unfolding. This will give you laser focus and better chances at actualizing your goals.

Once you have your vision map, be it digital or printed on paper, paste it in a conspicuous place where it will serve as a constant reminder, and then it will become easier to act on it. However, we must be careful of distractions that may seem like incredibly good opportunities but may derail us from our set goals and vision.

For some of us, we already feel like we are at the end of it all, and if it is still not working out that is fine. Some of us are early starters while some are late starters.

One thing is crystal clear, it is never too late to start. You just have to take the first step to experience your best life.

HOW TO CREATE A VISION MAP IN FOUR STEPS

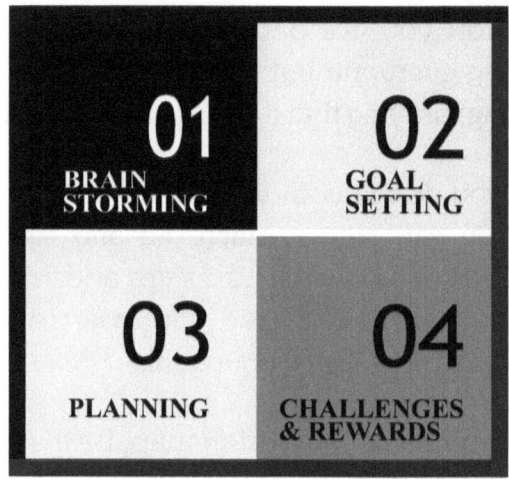

EXERCISE

CREATE A
VISION MAP

DATE: | **TIME:**

WRITE DOWN YOUR THOUGHTS

EXERCISE: CREATE A VISION MAP

STEP1 - Brainstorming
Ask yourself, what feat do you need to achieve to make you feel fulfilled?

_____
_____
_____
_____
_____

What pictures will depict your desired destination?

_____
_____
_____
_____
_____

What quote(s) speak to the inner person that can push you to attain your dreams?

_____
_____
_____
_____
_____
_____

Set a timeline with monthly or quarterly milestones on what you would like to achieve to show you are still on track.

_____
_____
_____
_____
_____
_____
_____
_____

STEP 2 – Goal Setting

Set goals on where you would like to be in different areas of your life, this may include career, business, finances, personal growth, relationship with family and friends.

_____
_____
_____
_____
_____
_____
_____
_____
_____
_____
_____
_____

Continue to brainstorm and write things down as you visualize them, then drill down to the most important goals. If you need to address multiple areas of your life, then you might need more than one vision board to make it more detailed. Also, to pass this stage, you must have SMA goals.

S.M.A. stands for =

S - STRATEGIC,

M - MOTIVATIONAL,

A - ACHIEVABLE

_____
_____
_____
_____
_____
_____
_____
_____

STEP 3 – Planning

- Go back to your itemised goals after you have articulated them.

- Write out your plans down to their most actionable points - this includes the steps, tactics, and timeline you need to achieve them.

- The more you expand on each goal, the clearer the vision will become.

_____
_____
_____
_____
_____
_____
_____

STEP 4 – Challenges & Rewards

Identify the next steps, envisage the challenges you may encounter, and fix the hiccups.

_____
_____
_____
_____
_____
_____
_____
_____

RICHER YOU

Identify your success triggers, enablers, quotes, and motivational rewards that will keep you inspired on days when you feel down or discouraged.

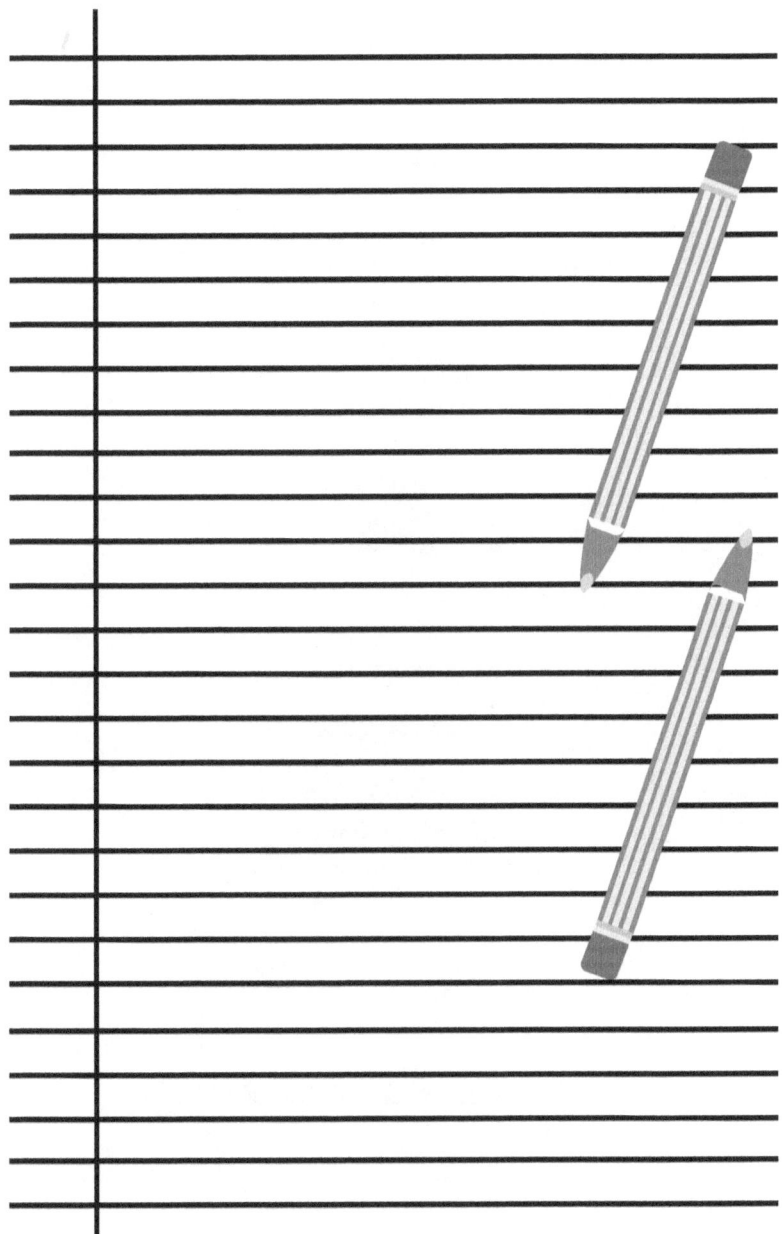

KAKEIBO

MONEY JOURNAL

COMING SOON

JOIN MY MAILING LIST TO BE
THE FIRST TO KNOW
http://bit.ly/moneyjournal

<u>BE THE FIRST TO KNOW</u>

CHIKA NWAGWUGHIAGWU

CHAPTER 6
THINK IN INK

"It's not how much you make but how much you keep, how hard it works for you and how many generations you keep it for. You could make a million dollars today, but if you squander it tomorrow, it really doesn't matter a whole lot that you made a million - Robert Kiyosaki

The Japanese have a money management technique called 'Kakeibo' - pronounced 'Kah - Keh - boh' and known as money journaling. It is a financial technique that has been practised for over a century and is based on the philosophy of mindful and deliberate spending and saving as a result. This simple budgeting journal also helps you get a better sense of your financial priorities and it will surprise you how much cash it has helped me save over the years.

A few years ago, I bought myself a car as a birthday gift and I was so proud of myself knowing my extremely humble beginnings, how far I had come and how diligently I have worked over the years. The car was sleek, the price was right, I even had some change left to get myself a phone as well and insured it. You can be sure that it is a birthday I will never forget in a hurry. I was so elated. I prayed, I danced and as I remember it today, I am still super grateful to God.

I know you might be tempted to say, "lucky you", but boy, did I feel unlucky! The car always had one fault or the other and I kept hearing these screeching sounds that I could not fathom the cause. I had my mechanic on speed dial who was equally milking me dry, knowing I had little or no experience with cars. Some days when I could not push away the uneasy feeling, I would leave the car at home and hitch a ride or even take the public bus to maintain my peace and sanity.

When I complained, my friends would say you know it is your first car, it is bound to give issues especially from the way you would drive as a newbie. Others will chip in, that car is fine but not suited for our roads that are rife with potholes. If you know the roads of Lagos, Nigeria you will easily concur. Other times, I heard a car is like a 'bae', you have to constantly pump money into it.

All these are caring friends, but they did not proffer any solutions to my problems. When buying the car, I figured it was a necessity that would make my life easier, not a burden. I spent a lot to maintain the car, and soon I realised my situation was bad, but I never knew how bad until I started a money journal.

Each time I had a complaint about my car that needed fixing, I recorded how much money I spent on the repairs. For every moment that a chunk of cash left my account that was outside my budget, I made a note of it and in a space of three months, you will not believe I had spent twice my entire monthly expense budget just fixing my car alone!

It became obvious to me that I needed a solution fast before I wrecked myself. I figured until I got a new mechanic or a permanent solution, I was better off taking a taxi to work.

For most of us, we know we are in a bad situation, but we never understand how enormous the situation is until we pick a pen and paper and jot it all down.

This may seem crazy to you if it is the first time you are hearing it, but journaling is an extremely powerful habit for several reasons. It is a budgeting and money-saving technique and the best part of it for me is the simplicity. No apps, no spreadsheets, just a basic path to success. Money journaling was not a social experiment for me but an act of necessity. I had to save myself from drowning financially and I know so many people can relate. You work so hard so you can enjoy life, but you find yourself living paycheck to paycheck and wondering why things are not getting any better. You suspect there is a leak somewhere, but you cannot put your fingers on it, and you find yourself confused and asking for handouts or probably maxing out your credit cards.

Keeping a money journal makes you more mindful and helps you easily identify those small details of incremental changes that seem to upset your budget each time. It also helps curb frivolous spending time and time again. It helps you focus on your spending and as a result, grow your savings even without putting your mind to it.

Handwriting your expenses in real-time can also be a reflective and therapeutic process and improves overall memory. Handwriting might be challenging for you, but the thought process is worth it.

Have you ever walked into a grocery store or supermarket without a list, or maybe you have a list just in your head? Then you will understand what I mean.

You walk into a supermarket intending to get a single jar of butter and you come out with a shopping basket full of things you never planned for but that seemed so enticing.

At that moment you are in the supermarket, you have this overwhelming feeling that you cannot do without the extra items on the shelf, especially those on a massive discount sale. So even though you never planned for it, you go ahead and get a trolley full of nice-to-haves and sometimes even forget the real reason why you went into the store in the first place.

With your money journal, you have to make a conscious effort and decide how much you earn, what you intend to spend, and how much you must save to achieve your goals.

Truth be told, some people do not struggle with overspending and can live a satisfying life with just the essentials, while others have the habit of spending when bored, stressed, unhappy over something, or even shopping online when they find it difficult to sleep at night. It all starts with window shopping and before long the cart is FULL.

Money journaling helps you set clear goals for your money. It is not about frugal living but conscious living and helps you ask some important questions:

- Do I need it or is it just a nice-to-have?
- How do I feel about buying it?
- If it is a happy emotion, how long will the excitement last?
- Am I sacrificing my needs for a want?
- Based on my financial situation, can I afford this item?

RICHER YOU

EXERCISE

START A MONEY JOURNAL

DATE: | **TIME:**

TAKE THE EXERCISE

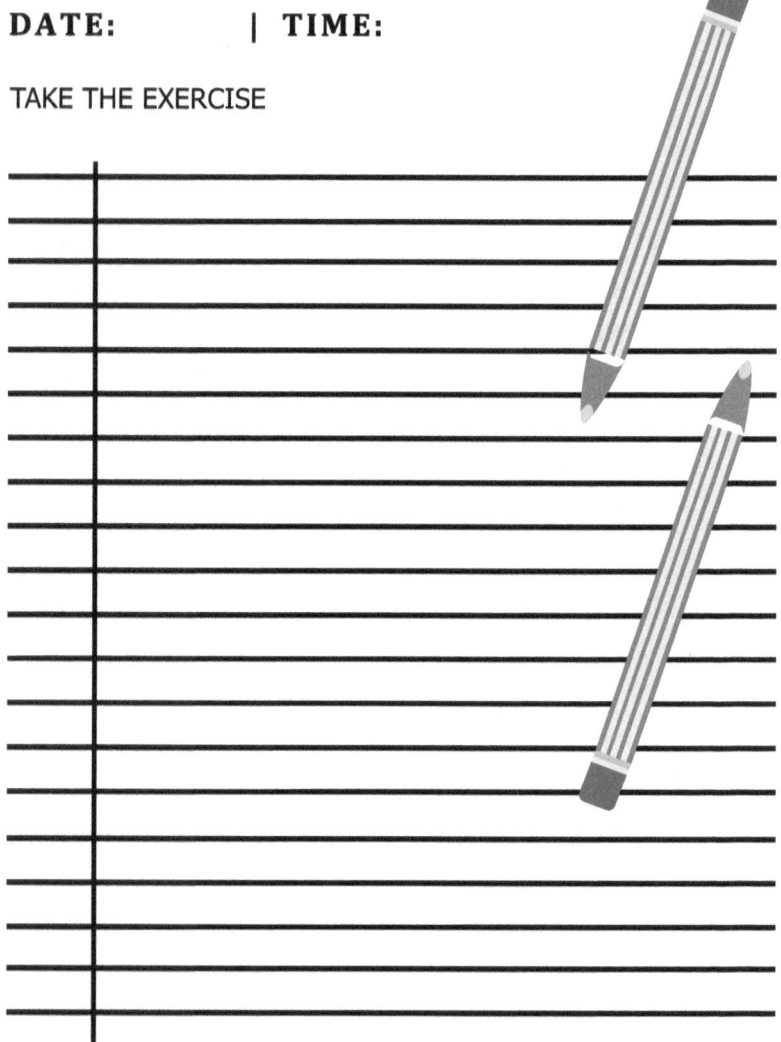

EXERCISE: START A MONEY JOURNAL

Get a pen and paper or, if you prefer, a digital notebook.

Calculate your monthly income and subtract your fixed expenses

- Rent
- Mortgage,
- Light and water bills
- and whatever fixed expenses you may have.

_____
_____
_____
_____
_____
_____
_____

Set and subtract your savings goal for the month.

_____
_____
_____
_____
_____
_____
_____
_____

List your spending categories for the rest of your money and include the cost or purchase value.

_____
_____
_____
_____

Needs: essentials like: housing, groceries, and the likes.

Wants: hobbies, hangouts, eating out at a restaurant.

Culture: books, concerts, cinema, visits to an art gallery or museum.

Unexpected: unplanned emergencies, home repairs, medical bills, car repairs.

_____
_____
_____
_____
_____
_____
_____
_____
_____
_____
_____

Going forward, categorize everything you purchase under these columns or pillars. This sorting process is golden and helps you to appreciate your spending habits better. At a glimpse, you can easily tell:

How much money you have

_____
_____
_____
_____

The total amount you would like to save

_____
_____
_____
_____
_____

How much money you are spending and in which category.

_____
_____
_____
_____
_____
_____
_____
_____

RICHER YOU

How and where you need to improve

FREE GIFT!

**To say thank you for buying my book,
I would like to give you a free gift**

**DOWNLOAD THE FREE GUIDE
https://tinyurl.com/FREE-BUDGET-SHEET**

MONEY JOURNAL

KAKEIBO

COMING SOON

JOIN MY MAILING LIST TO BE THE FIRST TO KNOW
http://bit.ly/moneyjournal

<u>BE THE FIRST TO KNOW</u>

CHIKA NWAGWUGHIAGWU

PART THREE
MONEY DOES NOT GROW ON TREES

CHAPTER 7
YOUR MONEY STORY

Money is one of the biggest things people worry about, so you are not alone. We all have something that keeps us awake at night that we wish would just go away by the time we awake the next day. While some people have incredibly positive money stories and grew up in progressive families, many of us grew up in homes where money was a taboo subject only discussed in hushed tones amongst adults or not even discussed at all.

We have all heard some money stories, false notions, and myths that have affected the way we feel about money. One such myth is that 'money does not grow on trees.' I heard this very often growing up and I am sure you heard it too. Myths like this one, and several others, are widely and strongly used expressions used to depict money as a limited resource, hard to come by and therefore something that must not be spent carelessly. This may sound reasonable, but is it?

When a parent asks their child, "don't you know money does not grow on trees?" or, "do you think I am made of money?" what they are doing, is filling their children with negative emotions about money. It implants the idea that they will never have enough money, that certain things are unattainable by people of their social status, that they are poor, they are average, etc. Such conditioning may breed extreme miserly behaviour instead of a mind of abundance.

There are other misconceptions I have heard that made me feel guilty for wanting to think about money and wealth creation. But today, I know better than what these myths suggest. Look at just a few:

- Rich people are dishonest – the truth is that people can be dishonest whether they are rich or poor. However, there are lots of rich people who made their money honestly and you will discover this as you read on.

- Money is the root of all evil - money is the root of purposeful living while getting rich quick syndrome is the root of all evil.

- You must be rich to invest - you can start investing today with as little as $10 or less starting with a high-interest savings account.

- Wealth is a product of luck and fervent prayers- well you should know my answer on that one already. However, one thing is certain, even God recognises and applies principles.

Even so, as important as money has been for generations, money management is not taught as widely as other topics in schools, religious places, or social gatherings. This may be because our parents or teachers did not know enough to share about the topic, or they are still struggling with their money troubles and fears. As a result of this lack of money knowledge, we all go around with these stories and myths ringing in our heads and unconsciously act out these scripts in our minds as we grow.

REWRITE YOUR MONEY STORY

Your money story consists of the things you tell yourself about money. It makes up your beliefs, thoughts, and feelings, and affects your behaviour towards money as you journey through life. Your money story is foundational to how you think about money, how you react to money, and how you communicate about money. Our money habits are formed as early as age three to seven years, and they stem mostly from what we heard during our parents' fights and arguments about money or the tense atmosphere that existed in our home when it was close to payday or time to pay school fees.

Children are like sponges and at that early age, they absorb, observe and mirror habits passed down by their parents. Their attitude towards money is shaped by their family background and upbringing and these experiences may stick with them for life unknowingly forming their money scripts.

Some of these scripts are supportive, positive, and balanced while some are sad, filled with fear and confusion because money is seen as a source of contention around the home.

Hearing questions such as "don't you know that money is hard to come by?" as a child, may have left you thinking of lack, scarcity, and poverty. In no time, you unknowingly became comfortable with the fact that you will never have enough and may need to manage and work extra hard to make money all your life. This cycle will continue until one person embraces a transformational mindset and is determined to rewrite the story.

It is sad to note that most of us have become victims of our past and have even become a similar version of our parents sharing tales of woes and doom.

If this is your situation, do not blame yourself. We all came into this world with minds as blank as blank slates. Everything we have learned, we learned from our parents and from the environment in which we grew up. Our parents and environment shape our mentality about money. If we grew up hearing our parents discuss the lack of money and the poor economy, these are the things we most likely also think about money. Very few of us heard stories about the abundance of money.

The battle of wealth is first won in the mind before we can manifest it in the flesh. Take this as an opportunity to rebrand your mind, Money does grow on trees, and it is all around you. Ask Mark Zuckerberg, it is easier to be rich than it is to be poor. Being poor is so difficult.

EXERCISE

IDENTIFY YOUR MONEY SCRIPT

DATE: | **TIME:**

WRITE DOWN YOUR THOUGHTS

REFLECTION
Questions to Ask Yourself to Identify Your Money Script

What is your earliest childhood memory about money?

_____
_____
_____
_____
_____
_____
_____

Do you remember your parents talking about money or fighting over their finances, Yes/No?

_____
_____
_____

What precisely can you remember?

_____
_____
_____
_____
_____
_____

Did your father handle all the expenses or did your parents split the bill equally?

_____
_____
_____
_____
_____
_____
_____

Can you relate any of your present experiences with the money pattern in your family?

_____
_____
_____
_____
_____
_____
_____
_____
_____

Whatever your answers might be, it is not for you to blame your parents. Now, you can rewrite your story just the way you want it to be. But first, you must face your fears.

Rewrite your story now.

RICHER YOU

CHAPTER 8
FACE YOUR FEARS

The first step to facing your fear is to find a stable source of income and learn how to talk about money. Follow the key principles in this book and be brutally honest with yourself.

If you are married, talk to your spouse today – it may seem awkward starting the conversation about money with your partner, but it is important because in some cases, one person is a spender while the other is a saver.

Starting the conversation with your spouse will help you strike a balance and prevent the impending fights and disasters looming in the air.

KNOW YOUR MONEY RECORDS
Think about things like:
- Do you have a budget or track your expenses? Do you have any debt, and if so, how much?

- Do you have an emergency fund? What will you do in a financial emergency if you do not?

- Do you want to rent or own a home? If yes, which location and how much do you need to put away in a year and for how long?

- Are you currently saving for retirement? Are you happy with what you are saving or are you going back to your hometown to become a farmer in old age?

These questions are difficult because you may not even have answers to them now but sharing them with your partner makes it easier to ponder and find a solution together.

Talk to your kids about money using simple examples and be a living example. Make learning fun and teach them how to earn their allowance money by doing simple chores around the house. From the allowance earned, peg a certain percentage that must go back to their savings and they will learn how to spend money judiciously.

Let me share a personal story.

Growing up, Big Mummy, as she is fondly called, was the bridge between us, children, and our father when it came to receiving and disbursing our daily allowances. This arrangement made it easy for us as we could demand it as an accumulated sum if we forgot to collect it on a certain day.

In August of every year, the situation became different. What was so special about August was that we had the August Women Meeting, a yearly fanfare every traditional Igbo woman looked forward to attending during the third quarter of the year. Big Mummy never missed it for anything in the world. So, she would leave us to figure out how to get our allowances directly from Dad which was not an easy task. For Dad, you had to earn every cent or kobo because he worked honestly and hard for his money - Saturdays and Sundays' inclusive - and could not understand our sense of entitlement.

We all got the clear unvoiced message as he was a man of few words, and as smart kids, we all set out to please. We would clean, dust, wash the curtains, mow, and rake the lawn, bathe and feed the dogs, cook, clean and remember to be extra obedient, extra attentive, and read our books in very conspicuous corners to ensure we earned the next day's allowance, fair and square.

Big Mummy would come back looking a bit puzzled at how neat, well-behaved, and clean everywhere and everyone looked, but we never told her the secret just so we could go back to our lazy ways after the August Meeting.

Little things like getting a money box, a piggy bank, or a clear jar for your kids will help them have a clear picture and understand the concept of opportunity costs when they have to deny themselves candy or chocolate cookies because they want to fill up their money jar. Tie the savings to something important to them like Christmas shoes, a toy they have been yearning for like a Barbie collection, the latest PlayStation, or college fund for older kids.

Teaching your children how and why they should save money will go a long way. Tying the savings to something they desperately want will keep them motivated. Do not be the parent who spends all your children's savings. You have been there, and you know how it feels, so do not do it! Instead, open a kiddies account for them and let them share the joy of going with you to the Bank to deposit money into their account.

Ask questions from the right people, speak to friends who are doing better with their finances, and get access to a financial advisor.

Other common money worries may include -

PRESSURE OF LIVING PAYCHECK TO PAYCHECK

With the high cost of living, high cost of transportation, our expensive lifestyles, economic downturn, worldwide pandemics amongst other natural disasters, the problem of not having enough money may never go away even if you continue to wish, pray, and hope.

You must take practical steps to manage money and not let money manage you. You must be brutally honest with yourself, try to live within your means, and do not let your friends and neighbours determine your lifestyle for you. Instead, determine how you can reduce your expenses to fit into your income and have something saved for yourself no matter how little it might seem at the end of the month, then grow it steadily.

If you have tried everything and you honestly cannot reduce your expenses any further, get another source of income. Start a side hustle – there are a good number of small businesses you can start with little or no money, no office space, and just your phone or social media account.

Think of a passion, interest, or skill people will be willing to pay for and market it. Everyone can command value! Think of something everybody knows you for or a problem everyone comes to you to solve and charge a token for it. You will be surprised how much extra you could make from it.

If a side hustle is not your thing, then put your savings in high-yielding investments and watch it grow. Remember you must first understand and gauge your risk appetite and lend your ears to the right information. However, a universal principle applies here: the higher the risk, the higher the returns.

Right now, you might be living on a very tight budget, but live every day by asking yourself what if my next pay does not come, will I be a giver or a beggar? That should be your wake-up call to stretch your mind and stretch every naira or dollar.

THE FEAR OF RETIREMENT

Retirement is a major worry for most people, unfortunately putting the thought of retirement off until the very last minute will not make the issue go away. Even if you are actively employed, at some point your company will have to let you go so you can rest and enjoy your golden years. But how golden will those golden years be if you have not sufficiently prepared for it?

The average individual wants to be independent during their old age, they would like to take better care of their health, enjoy life a little bit longer, spend extra on little things like spoiling your grandchildren, or even donating to a worthy cause in their immediate community, church or wherever their heart pleases. The last thing you want to be is a financial burden to your loved ones.

It is never too early or too late to plan for your retirement. If you are starting late you might just have to put away a substantial amount within a shorter period. My candid advice is to start planning for retirement from the moment you receive your first salary. Confirm if your company has a retirement savings account or pension account set up for you. If not, set one up for yourself.

You can do this even if you are self-employed. Take up life insurance, health insurance, stocks and bonds, index funds, real estate, and other long-term financial investments. This should set the tone for you to actively start a retirement plan.

You must take a serious look at your finances today and ask yourself if you can manage for the next 6 months, one year, or even five years without being actively employed.

In real terms, retirement does not necessarily mean that you are old, sick, and tired. It is simply a time when you choose to permanently leave the workforce behind and that can be at any age you choose 40, 50, 60, or even today.

If you have not saved enough for the future - that is, taking into consideration life expectancy, the standard of living you would like to maintain, your budgeted monthly/annual expenses, or you do not have an active investment that can guarantee you a comfortable retirement - you may want to seek counsel from a financial advisor or professional, but do not leave life to chance, start now.

Start now ... start afraid, start where you are, start with what you have, but start now.

EXERCISE

FEAR FEST

DATE: | **TIME:**

WRITE DOWN YOUR THOUGHTS

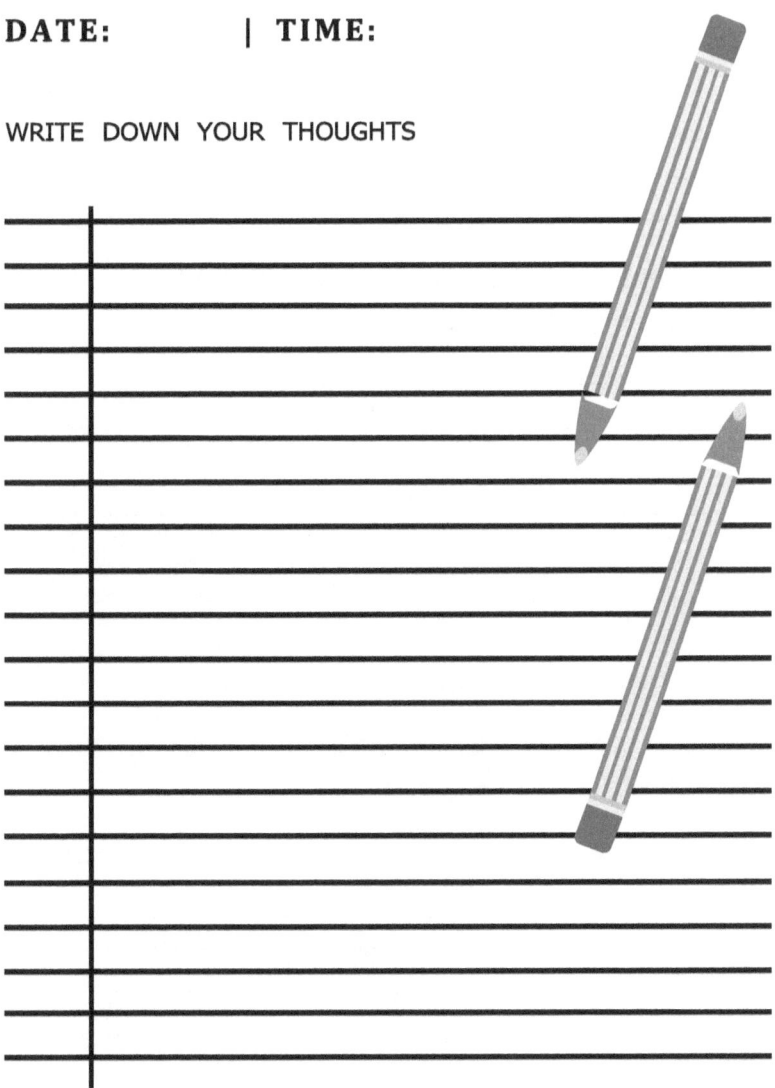

EXERCISE: FEAR FEST
Write down your major fears about money

_____
_____
_____
_____
_____
_____

List a minimum of seven takeaways from this chapter

_____
_____
_____
_____
_____
_____
_____

Going forward, what will you do differently now and within the next seven days?

_____
_____
_____
_____
_____
_____

CHAPTER 9
MAKE YOUR MONEY WORK FOR YOU

*'Money is a tool, tell it what to do.
Wealth is a journey, not a destination,
lay a path for it and tell it where to go.'*

- Chika Nwagwughiagwu

In previous chapters, we have discussed the many principles that must be implemented for a sound foundation for creating a richer you. Now, I will show you how much control you have over your life and outcomes because being in total control of your finances will ensure that you always have enough for the things you need and the things that are most important to you.

Imagine driving a car with faulty brakes or no brakes at all. Or driving a race car without speed limits or a steering wheel. I am sure you will agree with me that these two examples will only lead to a fatal accident, or at the very least major mishaps. I am sure you must have concluded that these drivers were quite foolish, reckless, or impulsive.

So why are you steering your own life without any form of control, speed bumps, or brakes to guide and direct you?

Having a plan for your money makes it easier for you to take bold steps and make big purchases like your car, house, school fees, planned vacations, to mention a few, because you can almost certainly tell where your next cheque or credit alert is coming from. It keeps you a step closer to achieving your financial dreams as you become more accountable to yourself, even as you grow your savings while keeping a tab on your expenses. Having a plan will show you where your money issues are likely to come from before everything gets out of control.

Remember that friend or colleague who looks good, dresses simply and elegantly, their kids go to good schools, you know they have one or two assets and yet you earn the same salary? You have probably wondered how all that is possible when you can barely make ends meet and your take-home pay can hardly even take you home. By the second week of the new month, you are flat broke, and you have creditors chasing after you wherever you go.

This abysmal tale is your story from month-to- month, and you cannot see any possible way out.

Well, the difference between you and your favourite friend or colleague is that they are living life on their own terms and are not bothered about pleasing everyone. They are in full control of their money, and they tell their money where to go. In essence, their money has a plan. Their simple motto is 'Where there is no plan, misuse is inevitable'.

You can stop the green-eyed monster right now and live the life of your dreams too. The problem is that you keep looking for a quick fix. There is no quick fix! You just have to take it one step at a time and trust the process.

Did you notice any peculiar traits about your friend or colleague? Look again and you will find out that this person spends wisely and can easily differentiate between a want and a need. Can you easily identify your wants from your needs?

Everyone's needs will differ but be true to yourself and do not miss the clear defining factor between necessities and frivolities.

Needs are essentials for survival, like food, water, clothing, good education, communication, internet, and transportation. While others are wants that are dressed up like needs, like luxury clothes and bags, dining out in exotic places, using the latest phones and gadgets, driving luxury cars, and the list goes on and on.

They may initially look like a need, but they will lose substance in the long run. So, whatever you place in your bucket list, just be sure that you need it for the right reasons.

Once you can separate your wants from your needs, you are halfway there. The other half is drawing up a proper plan or budget.

So many people flinch, begin to sweat profusely, and flee or even experience a mental shutdown at the mention of the word 'budget.' I understand you completely if you are in that group, I have been there too. There is no need to be ashamed, just acknowledge it and, for your sake, I will use a more agreeable word 'plan' instead of 'budget'.

Having that at the back of your mind, you will agree that when you draw up a plan for yourself, it should be something simple, reasonable, sustainable, and fun to stick to, and even motivating enough to enable you to celebrate the little wins.

Let me introduce you to my favourite personal plan, the 80/20 plan. I have been using this for a long while because it is not restrictive and reminds me that I am not penny-pinching. With this, I do not need to fret over my spending habits because my savings have been taken care of upfront.

THE 80/20 FINANCIAL PLAN

A personal plan is a summary that compares and tracks your income and expenses through a given period. For simplicity, let's say it is for a month.

While the word "budget" brings up a picture of restricted spending or being miserly, a budget does not have to be restrictive to be effective. A budget will show you how much money you expect to bring in, then compare that to your required expenses such as rent and grocery and others like entertainment or eating out. Instead of viewing a budget as a negative, you can view it as a tool for achieving your financial goals and strategy.

How does this plan work in real life?

The 80/20 plan is so effective and yet so simple to implement. Under the 80/20 plan, you take 20% off your earnings and put it aside as your savings.

You do this by treating this 20% as you would any of your other bills and mandatory expenses that you must pay before anything else. Then you can freely spend the rest (80%) taking note of your needs, and debts before you can splurge on your wants.

Twenty per cent is the minimum you should save depending on your total income. If you earn more, then you should feel free to increase this percentage to suit your lifestyle and financial goals. You can make it 70/30, 60/40 depending on what you find comfortable.

This plan requires a whole lot of discipline because no one likes to focus on savings. However, you can set a monthly automatic withdrawal to a savings or investment account you do not have easy access to. That way, your savings are automatically stashed away.

And by paying into your savings first, you are deciding that your long-term financial well-being is the most important "bill" you must pay. This approach increases the likelihood that you will save a substantial amount after a while. It converts the act of saving money from a desire or chore into a necessity.

EXERCISE: 90-DAY SAVINGS PLAN

Make a quick note of your total income for the month.

_____
_____
_____
_____
_____

Calculate 20%, write it down and move the exact amount to your savings account.

Try this exercise on the first day of each month for the next 90 days.

EXERCISE

SAVINGS PLAN

DATE: | **TIME:**

WRITE DOWN YOUR THOUGHTS

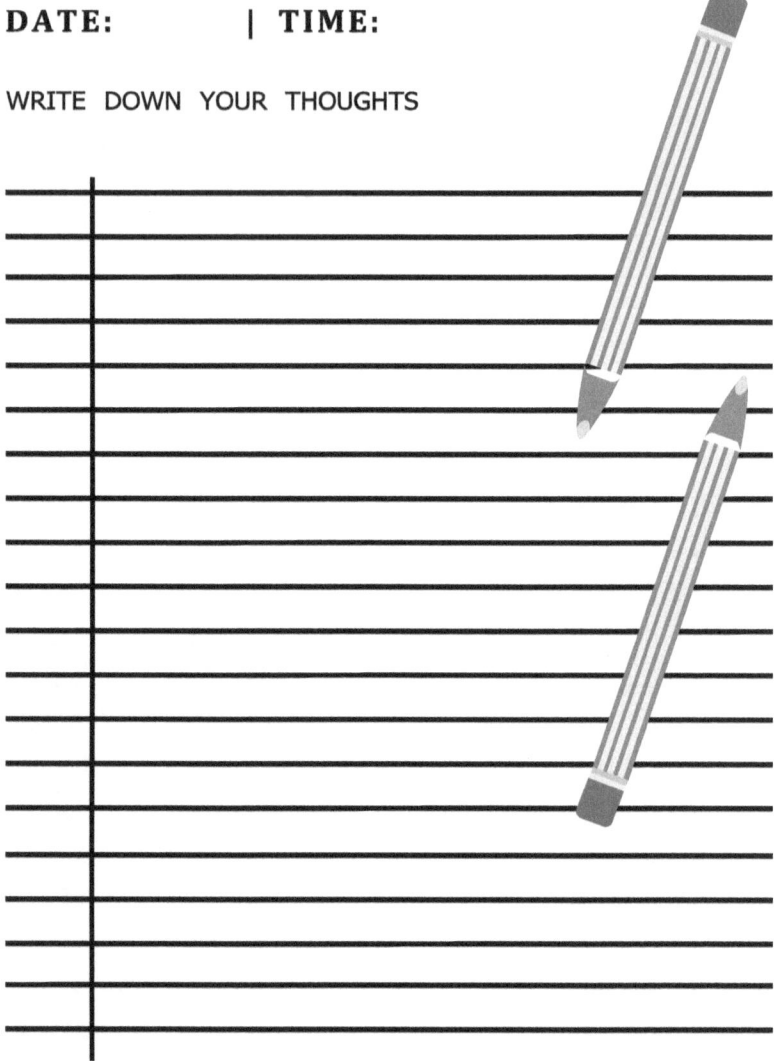

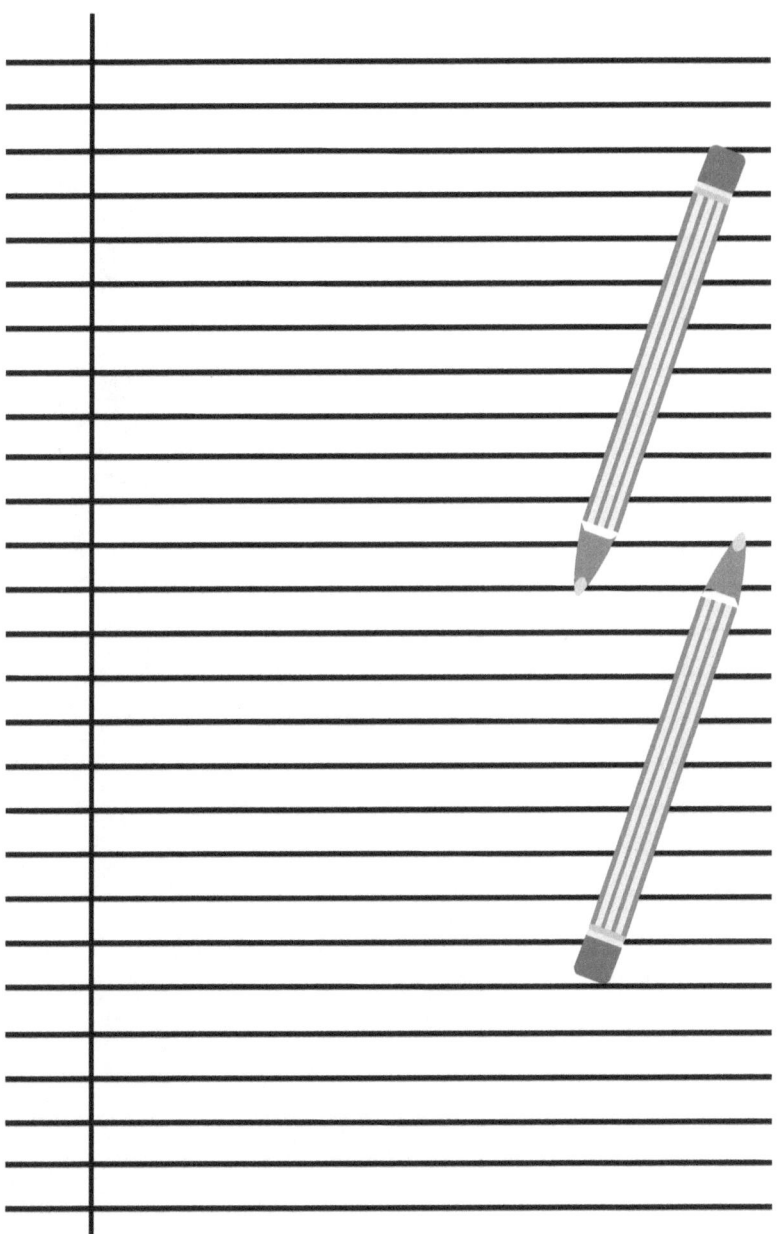

… RICHER YOU

CHAPTER 10
HAVE YOU HIT ROCK BOTTOM?

We all want to be rich! While the word 'rich' means different things to different people, we can all agree that whatever our definition of being rich is, there is an element of comfort involved. Financial comfort - being able to enjoy the finer things in life and being able to retire at a reasonable age without relying on the government, pensions, or your grandchildren for stipends.

And most often, having more money is not necessarily what makes you rich, but your spending habits. How much money you can keep and how easily you can multiply what you have in your hands is what determines your net worth.

Michael Jackson was close to bankruptcy despite making billions of dollars in his music career. Mike Tyson, one of the biggest names in the boxing arena, won multiple championships and made a fortune by boxing, yet he hit rock bottom financially.

You might know the stories of many others who hit the jackpot, won a lottery, or got an inheritance and are worse off today than they ever were. Some because of an economic downturn, job loss, but for so many others it is from making the wrong spending decisions and neglecting to seize the right opportunities or differentiate between assets and liabilities.

At the risk of boring you, let's do a very quick study of some of the richest men in the world and see if you can draw up some basic patterns.

ASSETS VS LIABILITIES TEST

Warren Buffett, chairman and CEO of Berkshire Hathaway still lives in the same home he bought for $31,500 in 1958. (Source - Business insider.)

Mark Zuckerberg, founder and CEO of Facebook, despite his status as one of the wealthiest men on earth, can be easily spotted out in his simple T- shirt, hoodie, and jeans uniform.

Carlos Slim Helú, the founder of Grupo Carso, has lived in the same six-bedroom house in Mexico for more than 40 years and routinely enjoys sharing home-cooked meals with his family and grandchildren.

Even celebrities are not left out.

Tyra Banks - one estimate puts the businesswoman, model, and producer's net worth at $90 million. She was once quoted as saying that 'While a lot of models were partying it up and going shopping and buying a closet full of designer clothes or staying at the top hotels during fashion week, I was at the DoubleTree or Embassy Suites, saving my money, and I bought a house at 20 years old, I was always more interested in experiences over things.'

She has been so careful with her money that at one point, her accountants had to set up a frivolous account for her just to get her to spend money on what they called "stupid stuff." (Source MONEY via Business insider.)

It is glaring that some of these ultra-rich businessmen and celebrities make Ebenezer Scrooge- the protagonist of Charles Dickens' novella, 'A Christmas Carol' - look like Santa Claus, right? These ultra-rich businessmen and women clearly understand the difference between their needs and their wants and the importance of accumulating assets and not liabilities.

However, I cannot guarantee that being extremely frugal will make you rich. I just thought to point out the need to set your priorities right. Reckless spending sometimes is a mirror of our self-esteem, where we feel the need to prove a point rather than consider our needs.

The main reason why most people do not reach their financial target is that they do not have a clear picture of what they want. Whereas rich people have a laser focus on their financial goals and are careful not to be distracted by liabilities dressed up as assets. They are aware that wealth is a function of assets - financial, emotional, intellectual, and material.

ARE YOU ACQUIRING LIABILITIES DRESSED UP AS ASSETS?

ASSETS include anything you own that has monetary equivalent and any item in your possession that will be worth more than the actual amount you paid for it if you intend to sell it at a future date. It may be paintings, jewellery, landed properties, stock certificates, intellectual property, royalty, and other intangible assets and investments, cash and money in the bank inclusive.

LIABILITIES include anything you own that will lose value over time or will be worth less than the amount you paid for it if you intend to resell at a future date. It also includes everything you owe that needs to be repaid like debts and loans, credit cards, etc.

Now, answer these:

Are you acquiring liabilities instead of assets?

- Make a list of all the things you consider assets.

- Review your list one more time.

- Are there things you purchased as assets but by this definition you just realised that they are not?

WHAT IS YOUR NET WORTH?

It is immensely beneficial to have a sense of your net worth as an individual. One of the most important calculations anyone can make when it comes to personal finance mastery is figuring out their net worth as it is your best road map to wealth.

Net worth is an indication of your financial health and helps you better understand your financial position at a point in time. It is the monetary value of everything you own minus all your debts (everything you owe). In literal terms, it is what you will be worth if everything you own was converted into cash to pay off your debts.

...will it be positive or negative?

RICHER YOU

EXERCISE

NET WORTH

DATE: | **TIME:**

WRITE DOWN YOUR THOUGHTS

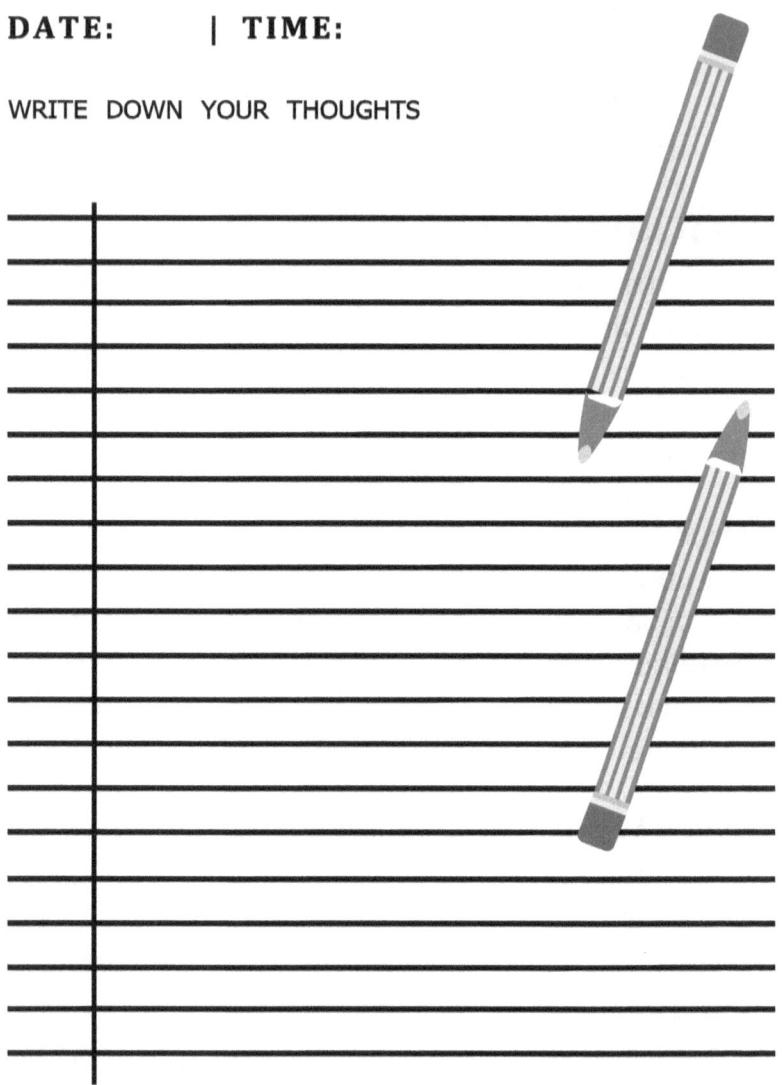

EXERCISE: CALCULATE YOUR NETWORTH

Take a break from reading this text for a minute.

- Make a list of all you own and group it in terms of assets and liabilities.

- Attach monetary values to each item and sum it up

_____
_____
_____
_____
_____
_____
_____
_____
_____

Subtract: Group A (Assets) minus Group B (Liabilities)

_____
_____
_____
_____
_____
_____
_____
_____
_____

SUMMARY OF ASSETS & LIABILITIES
=
PERSONAL BALANCE SHEET

SUM OF ASSETS -- SUM OF LIABILITIES
=
NET WORTH

If you have a positive value... Congratulations, you are right on track. You have a positive net worth.

If you have a negative value, You need to up your game! You have a negative net worth.

___
___
___
___
___
___
___
___
___
___
___
___
___
___
___
___

CHAPTER 11
THE 1 HABIT: CREATE VALUE

There was once a cheerful beggar who spent his days sitting under an old palm tree at the side of a dusty road path that led into a bustling town.

He spent most of his days rattling an old tin can hoping that passers-by would feel compassion and offer him alms. Yet, at the end of each day, he would only have collected a paltry sum, barely enough to buy a piece of dry bread and a bottle of water for that day.

The rest of the money he received daily was for a small jar of balm to soothe his aching joints from sitting at a spot all day and walking several miles to the shack he called home to lay his head at night. And yes, he also needed some medicine to clear his chest and nasal congestion from sitting in the dust all day, year in year out.

The man had been begging at the same spot for years, that he had become part of the landmark for travellers heading into the small town, asking for directions on the popular market days.

One day a wise man approached. Witnessing the beggar's plight, he called out, " my good man, why are you wasting your days begging in this way? Can't you see you are sitting under the Tree of Thanks? If you dig right where you are, you will discover a great treasure! " and he went on his way.

The beggar pondered long and hard and still could not understand these wise words spoken to him. Desperate about his impoverished situation, he spent weeks on end trying to find this stranger who left him no coins but words that stirred his spirit and caused him sleepless nights until, eventually, the beggar decided to take the wise man's advice. Using his bare hands, he began digging the earth underneath the spot where he had been sitting, but to his utter disappointment discovered nothing.

On the next market day, he left the shade of his begging spot and went to the bus park famished, limping, and looking for this wealthy and wise stranger and fate chose to smile at him once again as he caught sight of him, and a crowd gathered when they saw the famous beggar crying for wisdom and not coins.

This moved the stranger to tell him a story of his rich African heritage and the beggar's sitting spot under the palm tree which is fondly called the tree of thanks in his local dialect.

In summary, he told the beggar that the Tree of Thanks is the only tree of which every part is a blessing, no other tree is as useful and beneficial to mankind in all of history.

The oil palm tree is the only tree that can grow without needing watering or manure and remain lush for two centuries. The oil from its fruits can be used to produce cooking oil, soap, and candles, and its seed oil can be extracted to produce a medicinal healing salve. Its kernel can be used for road maintenance while the seed chaff can be a rich source of animal feed and the leaves used for twine and ropes. Its sticks for brooms, and back for timber, roofing, and the likes. Its sap produces a naturally distilled wine beverage in three different variants.

The kind stranger went on and on, educating one man and then addressing an entire community. When he was finished, the beggar began to dance with joy as he declared, Had I realized I was sitting on top of great wealth I could have eased my sufferings years ago!

I was once like the beggar, always seeking ways to fill the empty bowl of my perceived lack, believing that if I worked and saved hard enough, I would find financial security. I was not eager to leave my comfort zone and had fast gotten accustomed to the routine of doing just the minimum expected of me to get by day after day. Just the same way that I see you also sitting on your goldmine. I hope you have realised that it is time for you to harness the resources you have all around you and tap into the treasures within.

If you have read this book up to this point and have taken the exercises contained in the previous chapters, then I am certain that you have gotten a clear definition of what money means to you. And if you agree that money is valuable, then you are correct. If you glossed over those chapters, please take a few minutes to go back and read, digest, and apply the concepts one after the other to discover your goldmine.

MONEY IS VALUE

Wealth is infinite and true wealth only flows to a place of value. And if you have a job or run a business, then you have a clear understanding that your clients, customers, and employers do not give you money because you are punctual, tall, or smart but because you have something valuable to exchange for the money you want.

When you make money by working at a business, it is because you are creating value for your customers and you are earning in exchange for providing this value.

If you want to make a million Naira or dollars in X amount of time, ask yourself how to create value in X amount of time that is worth a million dollars.

That is the easiest way of making money and controlling wealth that is guaranteed. Money is just a medium of exchanging value between people. We spend money to buy value not 'things' as we are erroneously wired to think.

To Earn $X, Create $X Value.

Let's play a game. Get a piece of plain paper and a pen.

Now, name ten (10) of the world's wealthiest individuals who created wealth without adding any value.

I don't know about you, but I have thought long and hard and have come up empty on my list, however, here are ten (10) people who created wealth by adding value to the lives of others. As of the year 2020:

- **Jeff Bezos** was the richest man in the world as of the year 2020. He is worth $187 billion and is known for Amazon, the largest e-commerce giant.

- **Elon Musk** is worth $167 billion and is known for Tesla Inc.

- **Bill Gates** is worth $137 billion and is known for Microsoft Corp.

- **Mark Zuckerberg** with a net worth of $105 billion is known for Facebook.

- **Larry Page** with a net worth of $81.4 billion is best known as the co-founder of Google.

- **Evan Spiegel** whose net worth is $11 billion is best known for Snapchat.

- **Aliko Dangote** is the richest man in Africa with a net worth of $10.1 billion. He is best known for Dangote cement and Dangote sugar.

- **Nicky Oppenheimer** & family have a net worth of $7.7 billion. They are best known for their trade in Diamonds.

- **Oprah Winfrey** has a net worth of $2.6 billion and is best known as a TV host, actress, and author.

- **Kylie Jenner** with a net worth of $1 billion made her wealth from her company, Kylie Cosmetics.

YOU DON'T HAVE TO REINVENT THE WHEEL!

This is a clear indication that no matter your profession or passion, as far as you are creating value, people will break down doors to exchange their hard-earned money for it. It does not matter if you are selling a product or even a bright idea.

The first step to creating value is to find a problem and contribute your quota towards solving it. You do not have to reinvent the wheel, you just need to solve everyday problems, one person at a time.

Take another look at the list above, though they were selected in no particular order, you can see that the majority on the list did not invent the next rocket to the sun or build a robot that could walk on water. These are everyday people leading everyday lives.

The magic is to change your thoughts about money such that, if you want 10,000 dollars, instead of asking, "how can I make $10,000?" I need you to ask, "what value can I create that is worth $10,000, and how can I scale it to serve a greater number of people?"

The more value you can create for others, the richer and more financially abundant your life will become. The exchange of value is the foundation of the business world. Entrepreneurs who recognize this, hold the key to financial success in their hands and will make more money.

Wrong Advice: Follow Your Passion.

I have heard so many people say, "follow your passion and riches will follow and you will never have to work a day in your life." Well said, but what if like someone I know, your passion is sleeping for 16 hours every day and watching cartoons/ animations for the remaining 8 hours?

I simply cannot understand how that passion is supposed to translate to wealth. Unfortunately, so many people have doggedly followed this mantra without considering the economic value of that hobby or passion.

You need to ask yourself if that passion can be recognized as 'value' by many people and how much they will be willing to pay for it.

What pressing problem is that hobby capable of solving for others?

Apart from your family and friends, who else will pay you for your solution?

Your solutions need to be tailored to meet the needs of others not to fuel your ego.

Wrong Advice: Turn Your Passion into Profit.

There are so many things I enjoy doing. I am naturally restless and creative, but I had to stop myself from turning every talent into a business after I experienced several burnouts.

I would frequently tell myself; I do this for fun yet others who can barely do it half as good as I can are cashing out. I must jump in while the market is ripe. After such pep talks, I draw up a business plan, take up some short courses because I am a perfectionist, and roll out a business. However, I find out that something that I had enjoyed so much had suddenly become an unbearable chore once I added a business side to it.

I soon realised that apart from being a hobby I enjoyed it mostly because I could do it at my leisure without any intention to please someone, without any pressure or timelines or targets.

I enjoyed the total freedom it gave me and the fact that I had some sort of sanctuary where I could hide from all the chaos around me.

If you are like me, you will know this is your happy place, because when you are there you could care less if the London Bridge is falling. These hobbies should not be turned into a business.

However, some other hobbies are better enjoyed when shared with others like playing football or when done for others like fashion designing, music, these are better enjoyed when we receive admiration from others and so can be shared for a profit.

Passionately Create Value and Wealth Will Follow

> *"If a man is called to be a street sweeper, he should sweep streets even as Michelangelo painted, or Beethoven composed music or Shakespeare wrote poetry. He should sweep streets so well that all the hosts of heaven and earth will pause to say, 'Here lived a great street sweeper who did his job well."* — **Martin Luther King Jr.**

Success is not about your performance but about how people perceive your performance, and this powerful mindset has changed how I work and pursue success in all areas of my life.

Creating and offering value has a trifold advantage as you: hone your skill and become better; to the receiver, he enjoys the product and service; and thirdly, it is also one of the best ways to improve and motivate yourself.

Ideas are a dime a dozen and will remain infinite as long as the world remains. Look at Steve Jobs, Mark Zuckerberg, or Larry Page, who created extraordinary products by making things that already existed more awesome.

They simply did it better than anyone else who had tried before them, they put their mind to it, added some elbow grease and, as a reward, they had people lining up to buy their products or sign up by the millions to use them.

They look at the world as a market and are constantly looking for ways to make things better, faster, cheaper, or bridge barriers, provide information at lightning speed, connect people, and create communities. In other words, they are all looking for ways to provide value. Nobody can resist value.

You do not get paid for working harder. The secret is to provide more perceived value than you are asking for in price. Always tell yourself you are not just offering a commodity or service but value that will make the world a better place, one person at a time. Have that in mind and scale up your solution to reach and satisfy your waiting audience.

Cheers to a richer you!

NOTES

REFLECTION

DATE: | **TIME:**

WRITE DOWN YOUR THOUGHTS

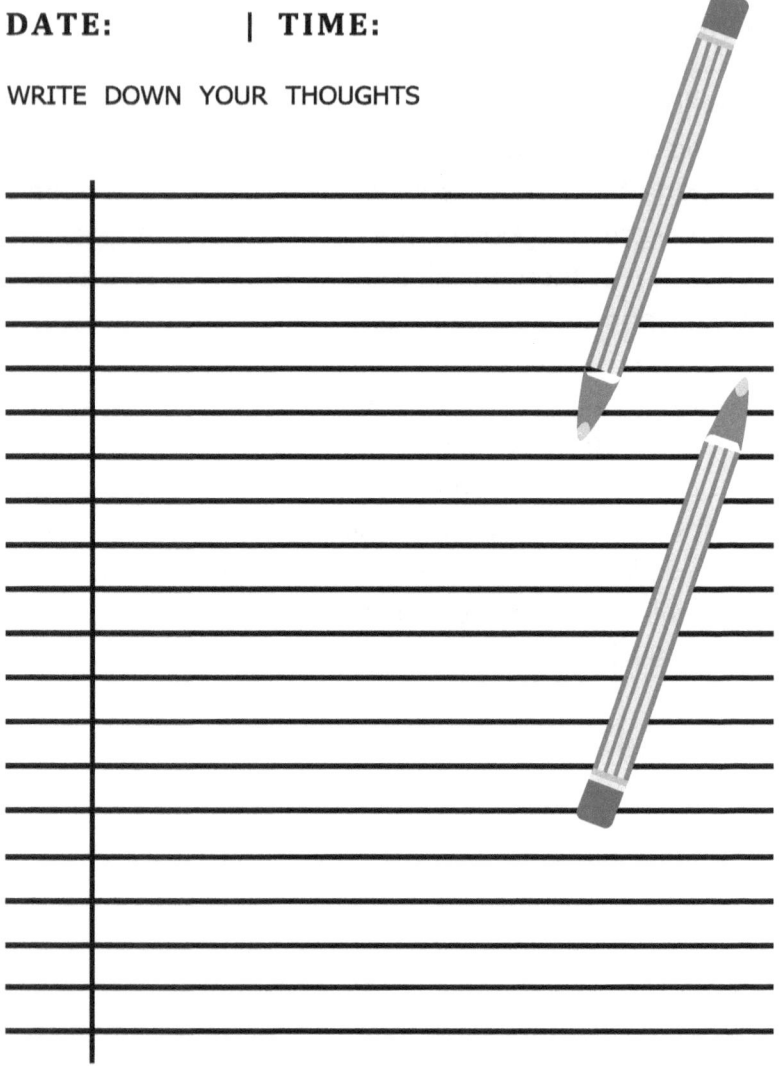

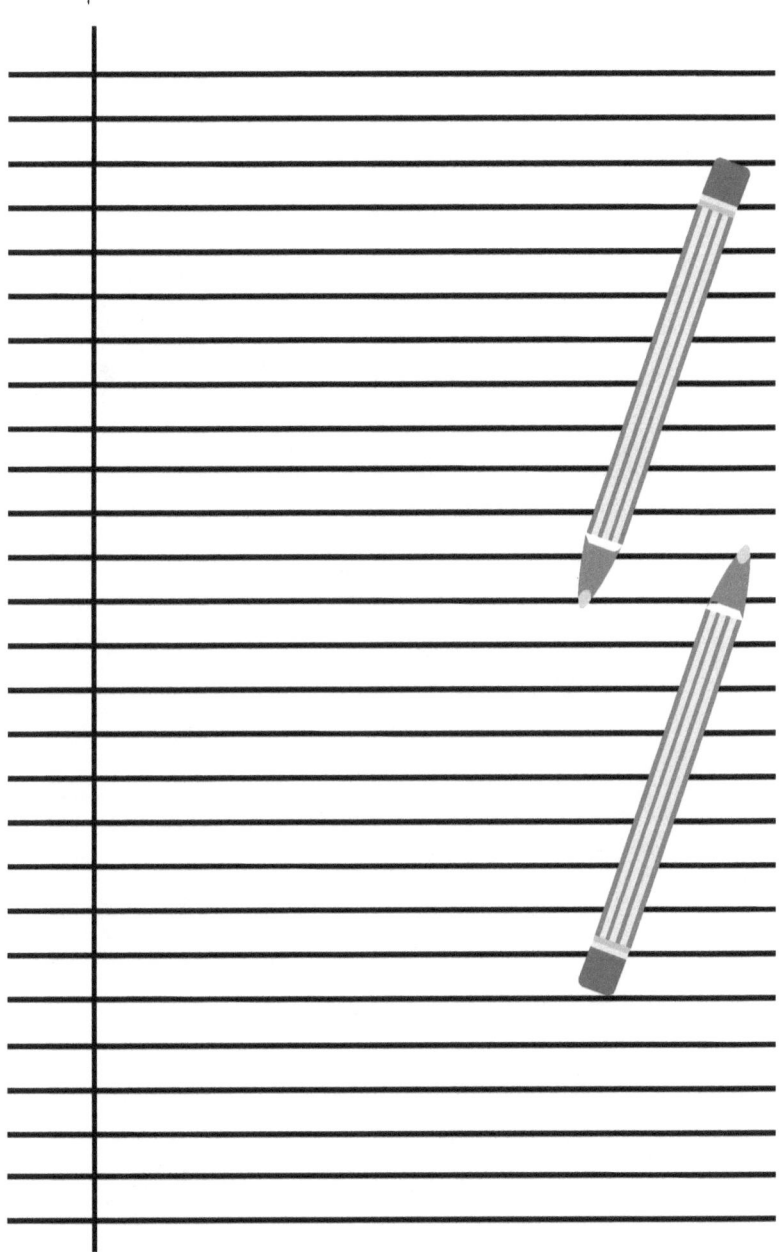

www.ingramcontent.com/pod-product-compliance
Lightning Source LLC
Chambersburg PA
CBHW031922240526
45464CB00021B/634